Wallace Drotts

252

Sermons on Prodigal Son

m at Kuma Schfield )
Scott

# HORNS
## and
# HALOS

# HORNS
# and
# HALOS

## in
## human
## nature

*J. Wallace Hamilton*

FLEMING H. REVELL COMPANY

To

The Staff, Officers, and Congregation

of

Pasadena Community Church
who, though very human, have more than their share
of halos.

# CONTENTS

Foreword, 9
THIS IS THE LIFE, 13
SHATTERED DREAMS, 25
THE GREAT LIE, 35
REMEMBER WHO YOU ARE, 46
HORNS AND HALOS IN HUMAN NATURE, 56
HOW FREE IS FREEDOM?, 68
WHAT THE DICKENS IS SIN?, 80
FORGIVE US OUR TRESPASSES, 91
SALVATION—MAGICAL OR MORAL?, 104
WASTE, WANT, AND WORTHINESS, 116
THE MIRACLE IN THE HEART, 128
THE SORROWS OF GOD, 140
THE DEEP ROOTS OF JOY, 153
THAT FELLOW WHO STAYED AT HOME, 163

# FOREWORD

THIS MAY BE, for some of you, an unsatisfying book.

It takes a certain arrogance to dissect a rose, analyze a sunbeam, or break a parable into sermons. But every minister is tormented by the encroachment of Secularism on human life, and seeks by every device of language to call men back to the soul's true home.

G. K. Chesterton once said, "There are two ways of getting home; one is to stay there, and the other is to walk around the whole world until you come back." This book is an attempt to follow that "walk around the whole world"—the disillusionments of the Far Country—the misuse of freedom, the sad gaiety of the happiness seekers—the waste of wandering— and all the frustrations of modern men who, like the prodigal, have tried to live apart from the Father's house.

It is written in hope that through its pages some may find their way home.

# HORNS
## and
# HALOS

# THIS IS THE LIFE

*And he said, a certain man had two sons.*
LUKE 15:11.

THE GREAT TRUTH at the center of the story of the prodigal son is one which is usually overlooked. This boy left home one day in eager search for something, only to return home another day and find there what he was seeking. In his father's house, he discovered what he had so vainly sought in the far country —right there in the spot from which he had run away.

That is a truth which is being vividly underlined today, in many areas of life and in the experiences of many living people. A few years ago it was poetically illustrated in a book called *Random Harvest* by James Hilton. Mr. Hilton has a superb genius for this: he knows how to take the thoughts and hopes and moods of a generation and, without talking about them, weave them subtly into a story. *Lost Horizon*, with its mythical Shangri-la, was a perfect symbol of the escapist mood of our time. In *Random Harvest* he has caught up the loneliness and homesickness of our day.

It is the story of a man who, shell-shocked in the First World War, lost his memory. When he came to himself, he could remember nothing that had happened in that period of

13

amnesia. It was all blocked out. He meets his wife, doesn't know her, and has no recollection of her. And she, while her heart is breaking for him, does not reveal her identity. Fortunately, however, he is drawn to her, falls in love with her again and marries her. She guards her secret closely, hoping that some day he will discover it for himself. Together they build a home, and become successful in business and prominent in public life. But always his mind is haunted by that unremembered past, by the life he had lived, by the woman he had loved. There are times when vague shadows float before his eyes, when bits of forgotten memories come, only to vanish before he can lay hold on them and piece the past together. And always he is searching, searching, searching for a face, for the woman he had loved.

And then one wonderful morning, drawn by some strange impulse, he makes his way back to a half-remembered town and a half-remembered house, and there he finds her waiting —his wife whom, with his now clearing mind, he recognizes as the one he has always loved, though for a while he was searching, as he thought, for someone else.

Something like that is happening now in the experience of many thoughtful people. Shaken and shocked by tragedy unspeakable and repeated, they are making their way back to some half-remembered things, and finding that what they have been seeking in far places and strange lands was, after all, only something they had always known but had lost a while. It is what Whittier once expressed in verse:

> We search the world for truth, we cull
> The good, the pure, the beautiful;
> And weary seekers of the best,
> We come back, laden from our quest,
> To find that all the sages said
> Is in the Book our mothers read.

14

I wonder if that was in our Lord's mind when He said, "And this is life eternal, that we may know thee as the only true God, and Jesus Christ, whom thou hast sent." He saw this prodigal world, estranged from the Father, making its experiments, seeking life in impossible places and by ways that never lead to life. He saw men groping, reaching up with their hands for something, they knew not what. And He said, "This is it. This is the life, this which they have scorned, forgotten and turned their backs upon."

With that in mind, let us look again at the prodigal. Only let us not be spectators as we look at him. Let us see the prodigal son as Jesus meant to portray him, as the faithful reflection of life everywhere, in every age. This man was a seeker after something. Aren't we all? We are all akin to the prodigal, this far at least. A great, restless hunger is in the heart of man, a nameless discontent that will not let him be. William Blake illustrated one of his poems with the picture of a little man standing at the foot of a ladder that reached up above him and disappeared into the clouds. With his arms outstretched and his head thrown back, the little man is crying, "I want, I want." My little boy said, "Daddy, I know who that little man is. It's Adam." And he's right. Adam, "old man Adam and his chillun"—Adam and you and you and I, from the cradle to the grave, with our hands reaching up, crying, "I want, I want."

I saw a picture in *Fortune* magazine, so striking that I cut it out. It was a full-page picture of a boy looking up into the sky,  a model airplane in his hands, a strange light in his blue eyes, the wind blowing through his curly hair; and underneath were the words, "The Promise of the Sky." That boy was wanting something, like William Blake's little man. And the gleam in his eye is the spark that has kindled the great material progress of our age.

Perhaps you have read the story of a dreaming boy who ran

away to sea. He was brought up partly at home, partly by the street-corner gang. He left home when his father beat him; he left school when his teacher flung dull facts at him—facts far less entrancing than his dreams. At last he ran away to sea, away from the monotony of dingy streets and dull people. The ocean was at least the symbol of his vague, vast longing. Out there on the ship at least he was a free soul. He could watch the stars and think his own free thoughts.

Who will condemn us for our dreams? Not God surely, for He put them there as part of the original grandeur with which he fashioned us. It is utterly useless for us to rail against this discontent in the heart of man, or try with Buddha to quiet or suppress it. Desire is the great driving force of life, and while it is back of all our sins it is also back of our science, and back of all our temples with their steeples pointing to the sky. It's really part of the thing that makes the difference between the animal and the man. Animals, for all their hardships, seem to be content, like Whitman's cow. But man, for all his blessings, is forever in discontent; the infinite in him is forever crying out for fulfilment. The more he grows, the more he hungers. The more he is educated, the fiercer the fire burns. The more completely he becomes a man, the wider his arms are stretched—"I want, I want." God made him so.

Well, what does he want? With his arms outstretched and his head thrown back, what does the little man want? He may not know. Often he doesn't know what he wants nor why he wants it. Often he misinterprets his deepest longings and seeks fulfilment in strange paths. But here is the point. Jesus held that man was after something great: "Life—eternal life, that we may know thee . . ." That is what they really want if they could understand their longings. Saint Augustine said much the same thing: "Thou hast made us for Thyself, O God, and restless are our souls until they rest in Thee."

16

Now, this is why there is so much disappointment and unhappiness and downright frustration in the world. We are wanting something bigger than most of us are getting. We are made for something higher than we are reaching. That is why the prodigal was such a fool, and why all who follow in his path are fools. He would not examine this life for which he was made, this heritage for which he was born. The hunger must be fed, the driving force must have an outlet, if not in his father's house, then somewhere. "Give me the goods," he said. "I want to see life." And off he went.

In city after city, in sensation after sensation he sought life and never found it. The more he sought it, the more it eluded him. The more he fed the hunger, the closer he came to famine. The more he did what he liked, the less he liked what he did. The path was disappointing. It didn't arrive. It didn't lead to liberty; it led to tyranny with the pig's trough at the end of it. And he had to struggle back, he had to retrace his torturous steps to the father's house to find what he was seeking. That, too, is happening in wide areas of our earth.

Dr. Clovis Chappel, one of the South's most gifted and beloved preachers, told of the first Christmas Tree Entertainment he attended as a boy in Sunday school. It was in the village church, and everyone was there. The tree stood bright with candles and loaded down with presents. Santa Claus pranced genially among the people, distributing presents to those whose names were called. There was a young feeble-minded man there, a hired hand on somebody's farm looking at the tree with eager eyes. His name had not been called and his face was growing downcast when suddenly Santa Claus took down the largest box on the tree, looked at it, and called his name. A look of radiance came into the poor, stupid face as he reached out his hands for the box. With nervous fingers he untied the string and opened it; and then anticipation gave way to pitiful despair. The box was empty. Somebody had played a trick on the village idiot. *Is that what God has done here*

It is a terrible story, but not so terrible as the stories that come up out of life. This world is full of empty boxes, and we've all taken turns playing the idiot. What is there in half the glittering things we reach for, and spend our energy to get? Hands reaching up; empty boxes! "Give me the goods," we said; grasping them, we found they were phantom goods. "I must see life!" and it wasn't life at all; it was just pitiful staring into empty boxes.

Ask Isaiah about that. He walked into the crowded city at festival time; he watched the people, hot and restless, hurry from one amusement to another, only to come away with tired faces and empty souls. "Wherefore do you spend your money for that which is not bread, and labor for that which satisfieth not?" Hands reaching up, and empty boxes!

It's a long way from Isaiah to Walter Winchell, but Broadway and Jerusalem aren't so far apart in some respects. "The saddest people in this world," wrote Winchell one day in his column, "are those sitting in joints making believe they are having a good time. This Broadway street is full of amusement places trying to make people happy, yet its people are drenched in unhappiness." You see, the chief objection to so much of our modern gaiety isn't merely that it's bad, but simply that it isn't gay. The box is empty. There's nothing there. Lacking the real thing, we try to manufacture it. We are like the woman who took her child to the circus, and the little girl, alarmed by the strange sights and sounds, began to cry. Whereupon the mother took her by the scruff of the neck, shook her, and said, "Look here, I brought you here to enjoy yourself. Now enjoy yourself, do you hear?"

An army chaplain, hearing the boys sing "Pack Up Your Troubles in Your Old Kit Bag and Smile, Smile, Smile," lis-

18

tened a moment, shook his head, and in good old salty, army language said, "Your tail must be pretty well down if you have to tell yourself to keep it up." People who are really happy don't have to tell themselves to buck up and be happy.

If you want to hear the story of the emptiness and starvation of this generation's life most faithfully told, read the modern novels (if you can wade through the alcohol and the cuss words). I can't resist the temptation here to give a word of advice to parents: If your boy comes home from school using bad words, don't punish him; develop the talent in him. He may make a fortune some day as a successful writer of "realistic" literature!

Dr. Halford E. Luccock has suggested that we go through the gallery of heroes and heroines assembled by Hemingway, Steinbeck, Marquand and others, to see if we can find a character who is happy, or is living the sort of life that can possibly produce happiness. It is a picture of boredom so profound, of emptiness so drab, that if this is what it means to be emancipated, if this is what it means to be free, if this is what it means to see life, then certainly our generation is prepared to understand what the prodigal meant when he said, "I perish here with hunger." Hands reaching up, and empty boxes!

The reason we can never find life along this road is a very simple one. It all lies, as Carlyle said, in the greatness for which we were made. "This is it," said Jesus, in effect, "this is the life, life eternal." We were made for that. And if we want life, we've got to reckon with that realistic fact. We've got to take into account the fulness of our being, and the greatness for which we were made.

Take happiness as an illustration. Everyone is telling us how to be happy. Happiness comes through the fulfilment of all our normal hungers—mental, emotional, social, spiritual, all

19

of them—not just the physical! And if we gratify just a part of our nature, any part, at the expense of the rest of us, we make our own frustration. So that when a young man says, "I'm going to live my own life," and then proceeds to satisfy just the physical part of it, he is not living his real life at all. He is just overemphasizing a fragment of his being and leaving terribly unsatisfied and terribly frustrated a whole range of personality above and beyond the physical.

You can't make life go on the basis of materialism; it will tear things to pieces if you try. The hunger for what we really are is the hunger that must be fed. The driving force must have an outlet.

And that is why this story moves out into many areas of which we seldom think. There are all sorts of far countries, and prodigality takes on many different forms. Not all the prodigals are pleasure-seekers. Some of them are schoolteachers and college presidents who have tried to build a system of education around the idea that we are minds only, at the expense of the rest of us. We don't need to dwell on the frustrations we have found at that point—we, with our big heads and shriveled souls, turning our very knowledge to destruction!

And some of the prodigals are statesmen and rulers of nations who have tried to build a civilization on the idea that this world is a market place, and that all its issues are economic. Business, that's all there is! Wages, houses, markets, that's all! "The business of America is business!" Think of any leader saying that! We have built a false and superficial civilization on the lie that men are animals and can live by bread alone. And when the hunger for what we really are isn't fed it turns sour. It turns to rip the world to pieces to get what it wants. You can't push man down into the estate of the animal without getting an explosion out of it. If we don't take that into account in our struggle with Communism, if we

*Ch/ sor. – go the Xch*
*feeding the big*
*lie too?*

have no answer for man but a material answer, if we try to
make the world a thing of better wages, better houses, better
markets alone, and leave out the deeper hunger, we shall have
more years of futility with more hells at the end of it. We
can't escape the Life.

But the great thing about this story of the prodigal son is
that it ended well. Not all stories do. This one did. It is written that one day he came to himself. That means, you see, he
wasn't himself when he left his father's house to look for life.
We never are. We are ourselves only when we are within the
Father's will and way, every excursion we make into the far
lands leaves us with a sense of frustration, with this feeling of
unnaturalness and homesickness. That is our hope. That is
God's unbroken hold upon us. It would be a terrible thing if
we could feel right when we do wrong, if we could feel natural
away from God and outside our Father's house. That is His
hold on us; the fact that we cannot feel right when we do
wrong or feel at home and natural away from home. What
saved the prodigal was his homesickness. He never did become
naturalized in that far country; he never did feel at home there.
He joined himself to a citizen, but he didn't become a citizen.
He still thought of himself as the son of his father; and in
one grand, heart-breaking moment, the thought stirred in him
of a half-remembered house and a heritage and a face. And
he said, "I will get up from here. I will go back to that. I
belong to that."

Widespread in our time is this homesickness, this feeling of
frustration and unnaturalness. You hear it in the speeches
people make, in the little scraps of poetry they write, in the
heart-probing of great thinkers, in the wistfulness of common
folk. Never have the hearts of men been so lonely and desolate
and frightened with the feeling that, in spite of our knowledge, we have not wisdom. We have missed the way, we have

lost the path to life, and, somehow, we must make our way back to some things that have almost faded out of mind.

There is a good deal of Christianity outside the church; some of it is making its way back through a new appreciation of democracy to the faith which is at the heart of it. The desperate needs of men and the frustrations of life are driving men to some sort of faith and lashing them there. And when they find it, it won't be a new faith. "This is it, this which they have scorned, forgotten, and turned their backs upon." It would be interesting to go down the list of men who have come back—T. S. Lewis, and Middleton Murray, C. E. M. Joad, and others. The late Gilbert Chesterton, after wandering in far paths, came back to faith and said that he was like those men who had set off from the coast of England to discover a new island. After a long, hard voyage, they landed on the shores of what they thought was a new country. They ran their flags up on the beach, and then, after looking around a bit, the landscape seemed familiar; on further investigation, they discovered it was the same coast from which they had departed! Trying to escape England, they had run into it. Trying to get away from home, they had come home. So, he said, it was with him and with many like him. They had scorned Christianity as an outworn faith; and when they found faith, it was Christianity after all.

Tolstoy had the same experience. When he was about fifty years old he felt life growing stale on him. He went through a period of two years of mental torture. He was plagued with the feeling that life had no meaning in it. It was futile and empty, not worth the struggle. He hid rope lest he hang himself. He wouldn't carry a gun into the forest lest he shoot himself. Life had no meaning. Then, he said, one day, walking in the forest alone, he got to thinking again about God, and he found himself wondering why he should. Why should the thought of God keep popping into his head? He noticed that every time he did think of God his despondency was lifted. There was an uprush of hope in him, a feeling of certainty and stability—hope. And life took on new meaning when he thought of God. "So then," he said, "why look I further? This is it. The reason I can't help thinking of God is because God is here. And the reason life takes on meaning when I think of God is simply because it is God who gives life meaning. This is what I'm looking for. This is it." And he said, "I will seek God and live."

This is God's unbroken hold on our hearts. You can never get away from God. You can never get away from the Life. You can never get away from Him whom God hath sent. He will follow you, haunt you and track you down. If you take the wings of the morning and fly to some mountain of ecstasy He is there. If you make your bed in hell, in the hell of some sorrow or unworthy act, He is there. It is the Shepherd out looking for His sheep, not the sheep for the Shepherd. There may be times amid the rush of things when the question seems forgotten or held in abeyance. There may be times in the far country when the face of the Father is dim. Then comes "a sunset touch," or a night when the stars don't shine, or a fox-hole somewhere in which there are no atheists, hair getting gray, sands in the glass running out; and there will be a Face. It is when we are shaken to the depths that we begin to wonder who we are.

During the First World War some church folks in London gave an entertainment for a company of soldiers who were on their way to the front. When it was over, the colonel asked a young officer who had the gift of ready speech to express the thanks of the men to the people. The young officer rose, and in some well-chosen words of wit and charm, he expressed the soldiers' thanks. And then, as if seeking some words with which to close, he said, "We're leaving now for France, the trenches, and maybe to die." He didn't mean to say that. Looking around embarrassedly, he said, "Can anybody tell us how to die?" There was an awkward pause as though he had said the wrong thing, and a period of strange silence in which nobody said anything. Then someone walked quietly to the piano and began to sing the aria from "Elijah"—"O Rest in the Lord." In the quiet that followed, as deep called unto deep, every man's soul was making its way back to some half-remembered thing to which he always had belonged.

This is it. This is the Life. "Thou hast made us for Thyself, O God, and restless are our souls until they rest in Thee. . . ."

# SHATTERED DREAMS

*Not many days after the younger son gathered all together, and took his journey . . .* LUKE 15:13.

"NOT MANY DAYS after . . ." What was he doing in those few days while he was getting ready to be off? He was dreaming, dreaming a strange, wild dream. He was thinking of that far country and what it held for him. His imagination had gone prodigal before he did. In his dreams he had pictured the far land before he arrived there.

A wonderful, wonderful mystery are dreams, the life that goes on in the mind, the picture-making power of imagination. Everyone carries around in him his own private movie theater. If you could open the skull of a person and watch the flow of thought for any given half hour, day or night, the images, the ideas, the little pictures flashing on and off the screen of consciousness, you would see a stranger and more entertaining sight than you will ever see in any movie theater.

Dreams are the stuff of which life is made. All great things are born there—art, music, books, buildings. "All that we glory in," said Edwin Markham, "was once a dream"—a little picture in the mind. Garibaldi's mother named him, in his

25

cradle, "Italy's Washington"; she whispered it to him in his lullabies; and he came through youth to manhood with that picture in his mind. Beethoven used to wander in the woods to get his music; in the studio of his mind he saw and heard great symphonies of sound dancing, marching up and down on the screen of his imagination. When James Watt's crude steam engine worked for the first time, he shouted excitedly to his friends, "You see it working now with your physical eye, but long ago I saw it working in my mind's eye." That is where all great things begin—in dreams, little pictures in the mind.

Take the dreamers out of history and there is nothing left worth reading about. Columbus dreamed, and a continent came to life. Edison dreamed and night disappeared. "Every great advance in history," said Dr. Whitehead, "has issued from a new audacity in imagination."

> For man is a dreamer ever,
>    He glimpses the hills afar,
> And plans for the things out yonder
>    Where all his tomorrows are;
> And back of the sound of the hammer,
>    And back of the hissing steam,
> And back of the hand on the throttle
>    Is ever a daring dream.
> *(Author Unknown.)*

But there's a debit side to this ledger. Not all our dreams can be trusted. Dreams are not solid things. There's a dreaming in which the picture in the mind does not correspond with reality. We call that "illusion"—"deception"—"a false show"—an image in the mind's eye that has no existence in fact. Our night-dreams are full of that; when the mind is free from inhibitions it paints strange fiction on the screen. Daydreams deceive us, too. We imagine things to be so when

26

they aren't so. "Why do the heathen rage and the people imagine a vain thing?" Isaiah, speaking of the enemies of Israel who thought they could overthrow the truth of God, said that they were like a man who dreams, and in his dreams he eats, but when he awakes his hunger is still there; there is no substance in the dream. The mind has enormous capacity for dreaming up illusions.

What was perhaps the most weird auction sale in history was held in the city of Washington in 1926. By special act of Congress 150,000 old patent models of odd inventions were declared obsolete and put up for public sale. They had accumulated in the U.S. Patent Office since 1800. Some of them had passed under the hand of Thomas Jefferson when he served as Patent Commissioner. A quiet, thoughtful man present at the sale said that as he looked over the curious conglomeration of sticks, wheels, glued wood and iron contraptions, the first thought in his mind was, "How fertile is the imagination of man!" One by one, these inventions went under the hammer. Some were clever, some were clumsy, some amusing—there was an automatic bedbug buster, and an illuminated cat to scare away mice! One woman had invented a gadget which enabled a mother to churn the butter and rock the baby in one operation. There was a device to prevent snoring. If you're interested in that problem, it consisted of a trumpet reaching from the mouth to the ear designed to waken the snorer instead of the neighbors. One man, evidently bothered with cold feet, had invented a tube with a mouthpiece so arranged as to warm his feet while he slept. There was an adjustable pulpit for short preachers which was operated by a release spring lifting it up or down. The auctioneer, in building up his sales talk, told how one preacher in Ohio, using the adjustable pulpit while preaching a sermon on the

27

subject, "Where Will You Spend Eternity?" happened to touch the spring at the wrong moment, and down he went!

Now, to some people, the sale of 150,000 old patent models would mean 150,000 laughs. But the quiet, thoughtful man who watched the hammer fall and heard the auctioneer's "Going—going—gone!" said he couldn't laugh. He knew he was looking at 150,000 broken dreams. He was thinking of the long days and nights of tedious toil, of the people who first imagined, then made, then vainly waited for the child of their brain to bring them fortune. Some died in poverty, still trying to market their inventions. He was thinking of the thousands of people dreaming dreams that would never come true, and he wrote it up in a poignant story under the title, "The Shattered Dreams of a Century."

In how many fields other than invention could the same story be written? This world is full of shattered dreams, of people imagining vain things; of economic illusions, political utopias, philosophical imaginings; of ideas in the mind that have no hope of coming true.

Part of the eternal fascination of this best-loved parable of Jesus lies right here. It is a mirror of all mankind, a faithful reflection of the proneness of the human heart to self-deception. Vividly sketched against a background of divine reality is this unforgettable story of a boy dreaming a dream that could never come true, holding in his mind a pleasing image that had no substance in reality. It's an old dream, as old as the Garden of Eden with its luscious forbidden fruit so pleasing to the eye, the fascinating dream of the hedonist in all the ages of time. Aristippus made a school for it in Cyrene; the Greeks debated endlessly about it, and long before them was the writer of Ecclesiastes; Epicurus built for it a cautious, prudent philosophy; and Philip Wylie wrote a plea for it in 1947. As old, as deeprooted as that is the persistent illusion

28

*that happiness is what life is made for, that pleasure is the*
*highest good, that satisfaction of the senses is the end and*
*essence of existence.* Millions of people have dreamed that in-
triguing dream, and in many forms and variations dream it
still. It has never been more alluringly presented than in the
lovely, lacelike poetry of Omar Khayyám:

> Come, fill the Cup. . . . Waste not your Hour . . .

> Better be jocund with the fruitful Grape
> Than sadden after none, or bitter Fruit.

In some of the loveliest language in literature, this poet of
Persia presents the philosophy of the prodigal. You "take the
cash and let the credit go, nor heed the rumble of a distant
drum." You don't trouble your mind about the future—
"Who knows?" Nor about the past, for who can change it?
"The Moving Finger writes, and having writ, moves on
. . . Neither tears nor wit can cancel out a line of it." You
don't pain your mind about the vast riddle of life's meaning:

> Myself when young did eagerly frequent
> Doctor and Saint, and heard great argument,
> About it and about: but evermore
> Came out by the same door wherein I went.

This moment, however, you can seize:

> A Book of Verses underneath the Bough,
> A Jug of Wine, a Loaf of Bread—and Thou . . .

That's paradise. The prodigal's young blood tingled with
the thought of it, and in his mind he pictured it and dreamed
the age-old dream.

It couldn't happen at home, not here under his father's
roof, not in this prison house. The old man's ideas were stuffy,
and the elder brother was a grouch. The far country, away

29

from the father's house, away from restraints and dull conventions—there! He must go there, and be clear of the father.

So say all the modern hedonists. We've had scores of books in recent years from the prophets of "the new morality," telling us that the "instinctual man"—whatever that is—must have the courage to throw off his back the unnatural restraints of religion and the conventions of a "corset civilization." The idea in most of them is that the Christian religion, indeed all religion, has proved an impediment to the full development of human nature; that if we could just get rid of priests, temples, taboos, revelations, we could be our own, clean, happy, carefree selves, free to live by the true creed, that man is basically a fine animal which religious superstition has corrupted. The sooner we start living by natural laws, the sooner we shall experience the glorious exuberance of primitive life and the sooner all the troubles of artificial civilization will pass away. It is a lovely dream.

Why won't it work? Why is the path so disappointing? Why is the dream so lovely in the mind, so elusive in reality? This boy wanted liberty and got drudgery. He wanted beauty and got bitterness. He wanted pleasure and got a pig trough. Why? Why is it always so?

Of course, the answer is that there is a Law. A silent, invisible imperative in nature stands up on the road shaking its head, saying "No, this is not the way to life." So long as we are merely dreaming the idea, holding a forum on philosophy, nature pays no attention to the dream. We could debate here a hundred illusions—the earth is flat, two and two are five, ethical restraints on human nature are unnatural. So long as we stand discussing the idea, nothing happens. But the moment we get on the road with it, act on the assumption and take the idea into life, nature pays attention. Something in the moral world, akin to gravity in the physical, stands up in

the road saying, "No, this road leads not to life but to death."
Why?

Some reasons are plain enough. For one thing, we are
mortal. Thrills play out, sensations are short-lived, pleasures
pall. And people who make a mission of happiness and stake
all of life's meaning on the senses find invariably that life
grows duller and not brighter, that sensation is like a drug
requiring heavier and heavier doses to produce it, until the
capacity to respond to it is exhausted. That's why there is
always a profound undercurrent of sadness in simulated gaiety
—a sadness like Pagliacci's singing with his breaking heart.

That is why the great hedonists of history are also the great
pessimists. Away back in antiquity a man wrote it down and
got it recorded in the Bible: "I tried it," he said. "I made a
business of happiness. I worked hard at the game, surrounded
myself with all the pleasures the senses could provide, withheld not my heart from any joy. Then one day I drew a line
under it, added it up, and all I got was zero, nothing. All is
vanity, a striving after the wind."

Would you like to hear it in poetry? Bobby Burns wrote
some of it:

> But pleasures are like poppies spread,
> You seize the flower, its bloom is shed;
> Or like the snow falls in the river,
> A moment white, then melts forever.
>
> TAM O'SHANTER.

The Persian poet too, this man who said that all he needed
for paradise was a book, a bottle and a girl friend, wrote some
other verses in what Dr. Buttrick calls "a lovelier Ecclesiastes":

> The Worldly Hope men set their Hearts upon
> Turns Ashes or it prospers; and anon,
> Like Snow upon the Desert's dusty Face,
> Lighting a little hour or two—is gone.

31

Thrills don't last. They will not last because we are *spiritual*, with many hungers, and because the things we hunger for conflict with each other. What the free soul is really up against in its quest for happiness is not the restraints of "the father's house" or any of the stuffy conventions, but the free soul itself, and the *total* self, with all its conflicting hungers.

Suppose we agree with the "I-have-a-right-to-be-happy" people on the premise that it is harmful to frustrate a natural instinct or to suppress the normal desires of our nature. Let us heartily agree with that, for it is true. All our God-given instincts are good, designed as they are for constructive purposes. But, then, somewhere along the road, life will begin to ask, "Which nature?" "What desires?" The self has many desires—mental, moral, and social. What about these? If it is harmful to frustrate one part of our nature, what about the rest of us? Happiness is the harmony of all desires. That is why the prodigal's dream can never come true. He could never get away from the rest of himself. He could get away from his father's house, but not away from himself.

For example, the alcoholic prodigal can't find his paradise in a bottle because he is trying to satisfy a fragment of his nature at the expense of another part of him that hungers just as fiercely for self-respect, social approval, and the affection of his friends. Why can't lazy people be happy? Not all prodigals lose their money in riotous living. Some of them get to Florida and to the seashore in the summer, with points of diversion in between. They flit from place to place; they must have the best of everything—the best food, the best service, the best entertainment. Every great hotel in every country of the world has its quota of men and women whose sole aim in life is their own personal, selfish happiness. Most of them are bored, jaded, world-weary, trying their best to satisfy their desires for ease and comfort at the expense of another part of them that de-

32

mands they be significant, that they do something creative and worth while. No, it is not in the restraints of the father's house, but something on the road saying, "No!"

These people, now in middle life, brought up on the Freudian school of morality; people who, as someone said, have taken the "nots" out of the Commandments and put them in the creeds; people who without moral restraint have gone from mate to mate in search of marital paradise, are not good advertisements for the dream. The awakening is not as romantic as they pictured it. The goods promised are not delivered. The roads that seemed so alluring have run out into dreary bogs. Somewhere along the road they ran into the rest of themselves.

A little boy, playing on the lawn, saw a butterfly flit from bush to bush. He was content to watch it for a while, fascinated by its graceful beauty. Then the idea got into his head that it would be nice to catch it, to keep it for himself. So when it lighted softly on a flower, he crept up and grabbed it in his hand. But then he found he didn't have it. At least he didn't have the beautiful thing he had reached for. All he had in his open hand was an ugly smear and a crushed skeleton of wings.

Some people think this is the very saddest thing in the world, that the joys of the world do not last, that even its loveliest delights turn to dust in their hands. But do they? What if there were no sadness?

There was a famous king in history who appointed a man to live in his royal presence, and say every day to him, "Philip, remember that thou art mortal," lest he forget his kinship with the earth. But doesn't every person need another daily whisper in his ear, "Remember, thou art immortal," lest he forget his kinship with eternity? That is what the sadness is —God's whisper. Suppose the dream should come true.

33

Suppose we could find happiness where some of us are seeking it, in the satisfaction of the senses. What if there were no sadness in the soul with joys that fade, no loneliness for that which we do not possess?

There is a Hebrew myth which says that when God formed man of the dust and breathed into him the breath of life, He gave man every treasure except one. He withheld from him satisfaction on this earthly stage, condemned him to perpetual restlessness, dissatisfaction and discontent with all things temporal and transient. The writer of Ecclesiastes had a shorter word for it: "God has set eternity in his heart."

Thank God, then, for the sadness. This dissatisfaction is the badge of our divinity. This sadness is the symbol of our sonship; it is God's everlasting whisper in our human hearts. And almost without fail, it is the door by which He enters our hearts. It was so with the prodigal. Happily, he wasn't happy. He thought his situation was desperate because he was so miserable. If he had not been miserable there, if he could have found life where he was seeking it, his situation would have been desperate indeed. The pigs around him were happy; there is no evidence that they were discontented pigs. They were quite content to be "instinctual." They were animal. But he was in desperate torment, and in his sadness he heard the whisper of his real heredity.

It would mark a new beginning for many of us if we could grasp this simple truth. You think your sadness means that God is far away, and it doesn't. It is the sure sign of His presence. Your loneliness, your discontent, your restlessness, your "fed-upness" means that you are not alone on the road—there is a Love there that will not let you go. There is someone whispering in your soul, "Remember, thou art immortal, with all thy hungers infinite, and restless will be your heart until you rest in me."

34

# THE GREAT LIE

*... the younger son ... took his journey into a far country.*

LUKE 15:13.

WE WERE RIDING along a southern highway on a hot August afternoon when suddenly Jimmie, the youngest of the Hamilton tribe, shouted excitedly, "Look, Joan, look at the lake!" He pointed to a spot in the middle of the road half a mile ahead. Joan, much more educated and sophisticated, answered, "Why it's nothing but a mirage." "A mirage? What's a mirage?" "It's something that looks like something but isn't." And so it was. When we arrived on the spot where the lake had appeared to be, it wasn't there.

Weird and fantastic are the stories about optical illusions, of which the mirage is one of many manifestations. Napoleon once crossed a desert on one of his long marches; the hot sun beat down on the long line of soldiers, tired, hungry, burning with fierce thirst, when out there just ahead of them they saw a beautiful lake, green palm trees, sparkling waters—a lovely oasis in the middle of the desert. The men shouted, broke ranks and ran for the water. But as they ran, the lake ran; the faster they went, the faster the lake receded, and then suddenly it wasn't there at all. It was a cheat, an illusion, a mirage.

35

A boy left his home, journeyed to a far country, and learned there about illusions. A mirage is something that looks like something and isn't. What was the name of that far country? We don't know. Babylon perhaps; Corinth, or Rome. It was somewhere away from the father's house and free from the father's will. That can be anywhere. Our generation knows where it is. We even know its name. We have coined a good many words in recent years—"fascism"—"totalitarianism"— new words to fit new systems, and none more expressive than the word "Secularism"—a word minted by an Englishman named Holyoake. There is a mood in the Western world, an ascendancy of ideas so marked, so widespread, so characteristic of this age that a word has come into popular usage to describe it. Georgia Harkness calls it "the modern rival of Christianity" —the new religion of man. Listen as she defines it:

What, then, is Secularism? It is the ordering and conducting of life as if God did not exist. It is the placing of hedonistic and cultural goals above and in place of those of the Kingdom. It is characterized, not universally but in startlingly large areas of modern life, by a superficial optimism and inner despair—and it has almost wholly engulfed our culture.

Yes, the new name fits the far country—Secularism, life apart from the Father, life independent of the Father, life ordered and conducted as if God did not exist, a colossal modern mirage, a great lie in our minds.

Many interesting analyses have been made of the rise of Secularism, the steady drift from a God-centered universe to a man-centered universe, as step by step across the past few centuries men twitched their shoulders from under God's hand, shook Him off, and moved out into the far land of Secularism—into life apart from the Father.

Some think it began with the Renaissance, in sixteenth-century Europe, when the power of the big Church was broken and the age of religion passed over into the age of reason. Some think it got under way with Darwin's *Origin of Species* —with Spencer, and the nineteenth-century humanists, who were happy to get a new book of genesis accounting for the origin of man scientifically, setting them free from the old concept of a God-created universe. But whenever or wherever it got started (and who can tell when an age is born?), Secularism has swept across the world like a plague, bowing God out and bowing man in, emptying the universe of Divine meaning and substituting human ingenuity. Renouncing the authority of the Bible, it has bowed down to the authority of human wisdom. In one realm after another, God has been dismissed as irrelevant—in the laboratory, in the schoolroom, in the council of nations, until we have an almost thoroughly secularized world on our hands; it is truly "life apart from the Father."

The Russians, on a tremendous scale, have set out to build a social order on a frankly nonreligious foundation. They boast that they can make a better system without God than with Him. Here in our own land there are millions who, whatever else they may think of Communism, would have no quarrel with it on that point; they too think religion has outlived its usefulness, and that God is wholly irrelevant. They conduct their business and order their lives as though God did not exist.

Lyman Abbott wrote a new "Lord's Prayer" to fit the new religion: "Our brethren who are upon the earth, hallowed be our name; our kingdom come, our will be done on earth, for there is no heaven. We must get our daily bread. We neither forgive nor are forgiven, for nature knows no forgiveness. We fear not temptation, we deliver ourselves from evil. And ours is the kingdom, and ours the power, for there is no glory and no forever. Amen."

It's a lonely place, this far land, with a feeling of lostness in it. There is a kind of terror in life's face when man is left alone with man, with no one to pray to but ourselves. We are uneasy and troubled in our souls. Thoughtful people feel a crisis coming in human affairs deeper than the headlines. Concerned about this lostness, even back in the thirties, Will Durant wrote some of his intellectual friends about the God who had faded out and the empty soul of Western man wandering in the wastelands, seeking something to fill the emptiness. In a sad and cynical book called *The Meaning of Life* he wanted to know why progress had proved such a delusion, why the optimism of the nineteenth century had given way to the deep pessimism of the twentieth, why all the bright promises of reason and the fruits of science had been exploited for nothing but futility or destruction. "We move," he said, "into an age of spiritual exhaustion like that which hungered for the birth of Christ. The great question of our time is not Communism versus individualism, not Europe versus America, not even East versus West; *it is whether men can bear to live without God.*"

You will not find anywhere a more apt allegory to describe the predicament of modern men and the great disillusionment that has fallen upon his spirit than we have in the story of the prodigal son—a boy who in his heart had broken with his father, set out under sunny skies to center life in his own will, to persuade himself that he could be his own law, his own providence, and in a far country manage life apart from the influence of his father.

It is a rather thankless task I have assigned myself here, to go back over the trail of Secularism and show why these two dominant characteristics in it—superficial optimism and inner despair—must in the nature of things be joined. How does the lie grow up? How does it happen that men can believe in the utterly false, and put their faith in illusions? You have to begin with that innate proneness in the human heart for self-deception. Almost all deceptions begin with self-deception. Whatever else the mind can do, it is certainly easily capable of dodging reality. When we want a thing to be so, it is no trick at all to convince ourselves that it is so; or, conversely, when we confront the hard truth it is easy to play 'possum, cheerfully convince ourselves it isn't there, and live in a fool's paradise of evasion. We sometimes mistake that for optimism.

A good case could be made for the proposition that actually we like to be lied to. We like the cheerful view of life, the prophets who speak smooth things, the voices that sound the optimistic note, the sermons that are bright and breezy and as brotherly as possible. The president of a woman's club, introducing the guest speaker, said, "Our distinguished speaker, Mrs. Smith, will address us on the world situation, and promises to leave out all the nasty things." That is how the lie grows up. We ask for it. The liar comes when we make the audience, and thus gradually we get what Plato called "the lie within the soul." That is, hearing only what we want to hear, believing only what we want to believe, we come to live in a land of make-believe, an unreal world of false optimism and self-deception. That is why we are push-overs for the advertisers, the utopias, and the lure of the easy formula.

The men who write the history books of our generation will have to include some chapters on deception, the lies we listened to, and the mirages we believed in. They will put us down, not as the realists we imagine ourselves to be, but as a generation of people who dodged reality, would not believe in unpleasant facts until they exploded in our faces; they will say we lived cheerfully in a world of make-believe and listened to illusion so long that it got into the stuff of our minds. They will talk about our isolationism, our Maginot lines, Pearl

Harbors, Munichs, the wars that crept up on us, with everybody meeting the dangers with "too little and too late."

They will have to tell how, in our age, the powers of illusion were spread over all the earth, how people had been lied to so often and so cleverly that they lost their sense of truth and couldn't understand it when they saw it. They will tell how a Nazi fanatic in Berlin, with an uncanny understanding of this weakness in human nature, adopted the whopping lie as his major weapon, believing the time had come for it and counting on the unwillingness of people to face unpleasant facts as the best ally to his cause. They will tell how Communism got a big lie going and beat it into the stuff of men's souls: how one country after another looked at a mirage, believed there was water there, until at last eight hundred million people were secure in the Communist dungeon.

Then, if the historians are men of spiritual insight, they will go on to write a more penetrating criticism. They will show how our political confusions were the manifestations of a deeper moral confusion, that the forces of destruction succeeded in confusing the world only because its moral mind was already befuddled, that the reason deception worked so well was because self-deception was already the set habit of our minds, that back of all the deceptions was the great lie of Secularism. Men had lost their spiritual vision and turned away from the wisdom and sovereignty of God to substitute their own.

Bring this to focus now on the area where the disillusionment is most dramatically apparent—the area of science. The secular age has put its trust in that—in reason, "man's wisdom"—in science apart from divine purpose, and the hope has proved to be something that looks like something and isn't. The twentieth century opened with an exciting optimism. You young people have no way of knowing the let-

down we older people are suffering; we began our years in a
time when everyone thought civilization was on its way to
millennial glory, and we are spending our latter years wondering if it can survive at all. What has happened to change hope
to pessimism and faith to terrifying fear?

When the machine first came in, everyone was optimistic—
the first telephones, the first automobiles, the first airplanes
made in the first nation in a brand-new world. There seemed
no cloud in the sky. We had inherited from the nineteenth
century the heady idea of automatic progress. Spencer said
progress was inevitable, that we were "doomed" to it. Everyone believed in the law of progress as thoroughly as they believed in the law of gravitation. Even Whittier, the Quaker
poet, sang:

> Step by step, since time began,
> I see the steady gain of man.

In that mood of optimism, the genius of man has revolu-
tionized the earth. There has never been anything like it in
human history. There is no area of life it has not touched. It
has put into every man's hands the equivalent of twenty-five
slaves. It has put millions of buttons under his fingers to light
his houses, cook his food, dig his ditches, wash his clothes and
figure out his income tax. Out of the brains of men have
poured these incredible, mechanical devices which, according
to a recent graph, have increased our mechanical horsepower
one thousand times. Great is the triumph of science. It has
spread its miracles over land and sea and air until the whole
"world is full of its glory, and the firmament showeth its handi-
work."

Here, then, was something solid to believe in—power that
really works, power which, according to the late Henry Ford,
has done more to emancipate man than the power of religion.

41

The laboratory became the "new cathedral of men's hopes." Where once they looked to God for miraculous deliverance, they turned now to science and machines. "Not prayers," said Karl Marx, "but plows." Where once they looked to theologians and philosophers for the meaning of life, they turned now to the engineers who delivered the goods—and the goods were power, profits, pleasure. It was not that they defied God or even denied Him. They simply ignored Him, excluded Him, left nothing for Him to do, as though they didn't need Him any more. Why bother with prayer or God's power when man himself, by reason, is learning how to do all that needs to be done? Listen to the humanists of our own generation: "The future is not with the churches but laboratories, not with prophets but with scientists, not with piety but with efficiency. Man is at last becoming aware that he alone is responsible for the realization of the world of his dreams, that he has within himself the power for its achievement."

There was a boy, said Jesus, who left home one day under sunny skies, journeyed to a far country and learned there about illusions.

Now the illusion is upon us. Now a black cloud has gathered in our sky. It burst one night in fierce fury over a desert in New Mexico—the ultimate climax of human wisdom, the end product of scientific ingenuity.

> We hung the ripe fruit of the Tree of Knowledge
> From a specially constructed steel tower
> In New Mexico, miles away from everywhere else;
> And the fruit of the Tree of Knowledge,
> Being dead ripe,
> Exploded and scattered its seeds of death.

THEY HAVE BLOWN THE TRUMPET, by Florence Converse. From *The Saturday Review of Literature*, March 23, 1946.

If the atom bomb has served any useful purpose at all, it has been to paint a picture against the wild night sky to dramatize vividly what has always been true, and what by instinct we should have known—namely, that the secular dream was a mirage, that what the New Testament calls man's wisdom (wisdom apart from divine purpose) leads not to the millennium but to pandemonium. The humanist's hope is an illusion, his trust in automatic progress is a lie. Science is not God. It is a tool, and a mighty tool which yet, under sway of God's spirit, may make the good earth fair. But "so long as the super-man makes machinery and the ape-man gets hold of it," so long as we go on putting power into the hands of men who have no God in their hearts, we have nothing to expect but futility. What is the sense of fooling ourselves any longer about that? Somewhere along the path the Western world has lost its way, and must make its way back to the spiritual realities out of which the richest of its heritage has come. Then, and not until then, will the fruits of reason be a blessing to the earth.

When we come to the area of cure and solution—or, if you like, salvation—we are confronted with still another phase of shallow optimism: the secular view of human nature and the lie in man's mind about himself. In the secular view there is no sinner and no sin. Man can save himself. There is nothing basically wrong with anybody. Human nature is essentially good, as Rousseau said. The only evil is in systems, in institutions, poverty, ignorance and social heredity. Therefore the cure for all our troubles is to change the systems; just give people a decent chance, educate and enlighten them, set them free from want and fear, and they will save themselves.

That is an illusion, a mirage, a pleasant, optimistic lie. And when we try to build on it we break our hearts against the facts. Thousands of good people outside the churches are con-

43

cerned about the world, and in scores of social, political and humanitarian movements they are earnestly trying to save the world. But they still cling to the secular illusion. They regard religion with an amused tolerance and God as wholly unnecessary.

> I fight alone, and win or sink,
> I need no one to make me free;
> I want no Jesus Christ to think
> That He could ever die for me.

So with no one but themselves to save themselves, they keep coming out with what Chesterton called "cures that don't cure, blessings that don't bless, and solutions that don't solve."

"If we say we have no sin," the New Testament writer said, "we deceive ourselves. We live in self-delusion." That is, any optimism that doesn't face the fact of evil in the human heart is too shallow to meet the deeper ills of human life.

Some years ago in Chicago, a barber's union performed a miracle—for publicity purposes. They went all out to advertise a certain brand of soap, claiming it would get rid of all the unpleasant things the magazines tell you about and your friends won't. They went down to Madison Street and picked up the filthiest alcoholic they could find. They took him to a barber shop, shaved him, lathering him, of course, with this certain kind of soap, shampooed him with this certain kind of soap, took him to a hotel that used exclusively this certain kind of soap; bought him a new suit, shirts and socks which were laundered with this certain kind of soap. And then in the newspapers they published their gospel of redemption, saying in effect: "See what we have done—we have made a new man with soap." The hopeful implication was, of course, that "whosoever will may come"—any man, even the worst, would be a candidate for salvation if only he had a decent chance.

44

About a week later, however, there was another item in the paper, on page 13. Some nosy, irreverent reporter told the sequel: "The man made over by the barber's union was found last night on Madison Street drunk, dirty and disillusioned." The story is common but not unimportant. It is a little parable of our day, of its shallowness, its refusal to face facts, of the distortions and gymnastics it will go through to avoid admitting the real failure of man.

To some, all this may seem pessimistic. It isn't. You get pessimism when you put your trust in things that deceive. We Christians are not pessimists. We have our hopes and we know where they are rooted. We are frankly and stubbornly pessimistic about all human efforts to save ourselves without the Saviour and to solve our problems without the Solution. We have no hope in education that leaves out the one great Fact that gives meaning to all facts. (Germany had brilliant education, and came up with a scientific savagery more brutal than Caesar's.) We have no hope in a social planning that leaves out the Great Planner. (Russia has social planning apart from the Father; may God protect us from it!) We have no faith in a psychology that has a method but no Master. We have great faith in education and social planning and psychology pursued under the redeeming, renewing touch of God!

*What is May*
*sp 92*

# REMEMBER WHO YOU ARE

*What is man, that thou art mindful of him? . . .* PSALM 8:4.

SOMEONE HAS SAID that the preacher's real business is to tell men and women who they are. People forget that, as did the prodigal son. He forgot who he was and wandered into wastelands and got lost in a far country of doubt and disillusionment. It is a terrible thing to forget who you are. There are times when it seems a whole generation falls into a state of moral amnesia and forgets what it means to be human.

A current story has it that a half-demented man was seen rushing wildly from office to office in a government building in Washington. He was flinging open the doors of closets and steel files, hunting in waste baskets, crawling under tables, peering under rugs. When finally seized by a detective and questioned about the object of his frantic search, he said, "I am looking for me. I am trying to find myself." A witty reporter, commenting on the story and the tensions in the national capitol, said that if he had to go crazy, he would want it to happen in Washington, for there no one would know the difference. It may be the man wasn't crazy. Perhaps that is what everyone is really looking for in the City of Confusion. Can anybody tell us who we are?

A sensitive Jew wrote a book about that. He called it *The*

46

*Search.* It was the story of himself, of his own life, of the pain of a man tied to an identification he did not understand. He had come up through many creative occupations—reporter, novelist, playwright, social worker, war correspondent. Yet always, through all these occupations, he was something other than what he seemed. Wherever he went, whatever he did, he was primarily a Jew in search of the meaning of himself, a man hunting his identity, an intelligence digging for its roots. And he reached the conclusion that what he was every man is —a bewildered wanderer seeking to find and realize himself. Can anybody tell us who we are?

Suddenly the question becomes intensely important. Who are we? What is man? The old question that haunted the mind of the psalmist as he stood wondering under the stars is pressing today with a terrible insistence. Back of all the political questions, back of the fierce clashing of ideological forces is the basic, elemental question, "What is man?" Is he a person or a pawn, savage or son, someone who counts or merely something to be counted? We can't escape that any more. We must know who we are as a matter of survival. "The struggle of the future," said Pierre Van Paassen, "is the struggle for man."

Here in the Western world we have tried to build our civilization around a concept that sharply emerges in the pages of the Bible, the spiritual interpretation of life, the concept of the dignity of the individual, the sacredness of personality, the infinite worth of the common man. We have said that the truth is self-evident, that all men were created equal, endowed by their Creator with certain inalienable rights. We built on that. We assumed that this was the secure, permanent factor in our social heritage, so obvious that it was self-evident, that all future progress must be along this road of man's self-realization under God. That comfortable assumption has been

47

smashed. Today we are encountering a terrific resurgence of barbarism, and not alone in our Communist enemies who frankly debunk the whole Christian concept and look on man with utter contempt, and who can succeed in their purpose of world domination only by a wholesale destruction of every single vestige of individual self-respect. But here within our own Western world there has been a serious undermining of those spiritual beliefs on which the democratic ideal rests. Secularism, which began by exalting man, is now in the process of debasing him. Secularists first scrapped the Christian idea of God and they are now scrapping the Christian view of man, and with it all that gives him dignity in the earth. For more than half a century we have been deluged with Darwinian and Nietzschean views of man emphasizing the animal aspects of his nature—ancestry, instincts, appetites—until man, the child of God, has disappeared and, like the prodigal, has landed quite humiliatingly among the animals.

Much of the trouble comes out of partial views, out of our habit of analyzing everything in piecemeal fashion, each seeing his own specialized department without relation to the whole —like the blind man at the circus who felt the elephant's tail and thought he had the elephant. It is a mistake to assume that science speaks with one voice. Bring all the learned specialists together and you have a Tower of Babel. Everyone speaks his own language. The depth psychologist won't speak to the behaviorist, and the cellulose chemist can't tell what the fuel chemist is talking about. All of these subhuman views of man with which our generation has been deluged are one-sided, fragmentary views.

The biologist looks at man, and breaks him up into cells. That is what he works with in his department—cells, and he comes up with the answer that man is "a complicated animal." As, of course, he is, a complex organism of living cells, billions of them, acting and grouping themselves in the various organs of the body with an intelligence unbelievable.

In another department the biochemist is breaking man up into elements—sodium, iron and calcium. He works with molecules in his department, and he comes up with the answer that man is "a chemical machine." And he is; man is an amazingly intricate chemical mechanism. The stomach is a chemical food factory; the heart is a chemical pump; the muscles are chemical engines; the brain, with its nerve lines, is a chemical intercommunications system more delicately adjusted than any telephone system.

One night I sat listening to a man explain how television works, how the camera with its electronic eye takes pictures in the studio and, by electrical impulses, projects them through the air waves. Everyone sat very still, gripped with the wonder of it. Yet every man there was looking at the camera through an instrument more wonderful than the instrument on display. The eye is a camera, a chemical camera, automatic, able without levers or operators to turn itself and focus on the view it wants, near or far, and get the whole picture in technicolor. All chemical, remember! If you went into a camera factory and told the craftsmen that instead of using wood and metal and glass to make cameras, henceforth they would have to construct them of salt, water and albumen, and make them completely automatic, what do you suppose they would say to you? Why should a man fall down on his knees before the Milky Way? There is more wonder in the eye than in anything it looks upon. "We are fearfully and wonderfully made." We are indeed fearful and wonderful machines.

The psychologist has his department; in fact he has several departments. He studies mind, and in that undiscovered land every mind is lost. Out of his department he brings his partial

49

views: man is a bundle of inherited impulses, he is the organized sum of his glandular habits, or he is a social animal, or "an animal that cooks his food." Every one of these answers is in some measure true. Yet every one of them is a lie because it centers on a fragment.

Will Rogers used to say that "nobody is as stupid as an educated man when you get him out of the department he is educated in." In the depression years a man who had lost almost everything he had walked down the street one day, and at every intersection thrust out his left arm. Someone asked him why. "That," he answered, "is all I have left of my automobile." Nothing left but the gesture! So in one realm after another these "terrible simplifiers" have studied man piecemeal, bit by bit reduced him to the level of the life below him, bleached out the spiritual, squeezed out everything but the physical, until there is little left of man but the gesture. "Man," said Berdyaev, "has disappeared. There remain only certain of his functions."

Soak your mind in that subhuman stuff, and you will soon take it for granted that you belong to a sickly breed, that it doesn't matter much what happens to man here on this spinning earth. Man, said H. L. Mencken, is "a sick fly on a dizzy wheel." If this is what human beings are—chemical animals, instinctual, social, producing animals—then what is wrong with Communism or any other anthill philosophy?

You can't bombard a generation with the idea that men are animals without getting animal behavior. You can't cut them off from Sonship and have anything left of dignity but a gesture. "Thou hast made him a little lower than divine." We have to get that straight again as a matter of survival. We have to see man where the psalmist placed him, against the backdrop of eternity. He has no dignity, no meaning, no worth apart from his Sonship, apart from the image of God in him. "Thou hast made him a little lower than divine." Thou!

50

"Drop God out of one end of the sentence, and man drops out of the other."

Who are we then? What is the Christian view of man? Of course, we must start with the animal. There is no disposition in Christian teaching to deny his essential kinship with the earth. On the physical side of his nature he is part and product of all nature. He is made of the earth, as are all animals. He feeds on the earth as all animals do. The earth is his native land. He can never separate himself from the earth. He can lift one foot from it but not two, and that not for long. It is this mystic oneness with the earth that keeps him close to it, that turns him when tired or baffled, with wistful eagerness, to Mother Nature. Tolstoy used to plow the ground in his bare feet; he wanted the earth to get up in him. That is why men go fishing, why Boy Scouts go on hikes. We are part of the earth. A ranchman said, "Often when I camp at night, it has made me want to become the ground, become the water, the trees, to mix with the whole thing and never unmix again." "The Lord God formed man of the dust of the ground." That is literally true. What is man? He is the off-spring of dust, a child of the earth.

Yet it is quite clear that on another side of his nature he is part of a higher existence. Woven into his dust are things that make him more than dust. He "walks up the stairs of his concepts" into a wonder-world of thought. Ideas leap up within his brain, imagination leaves the dust of his body to wander in a thousand fields, conscience whispers and he hears the overtones of a world invisible. Man is made in the image of God. That is, he has personality, and a nature formed after the likeness of God's nature. He possesses powers within a finite range like the powers God holds in an infinite range. "God has set eternity in his heart."

MacNeile Dixon says that is what the fine arts are; all music, all poetry, all the upreach of man's soul, all man's attempt to recapture the ideal is like some lost chord he is trying to get on the keys again; it is something in his racial memory, a remembrance of a perfection he was made for, once had, and must get back. Animals aren't bothered with it. They are content. But man wanders, restless, like a traveler in an alien land, in his imagery revisiting the country of his birth—or was it the country of his birth? So music, poetry, and the artistic outreach of his nature are the echoes in him of his higher heredity, the wandering of his soul to the borderland of the paradise he was designed by nature to inhabit. What is man? He is a restless child of eternity. "Thou hast made him a little lower than divine."

That means that most of our trouble comes, not out of thinking too highly of ourselves, but actually out of thinking too cheaply of ourselves. Do you suppose people would do the silly, shabby things they do to themselves and to others if they could remember who they are? "Made a little lower than divine."

One September morning a father and his son were on their way to Grand Central Station in New York City. The son was taking the train for a college in New England. Just for a moment the father stood there, wanting to say so many things but saying only one, though it was quite enough: "Bill, never forget who you are." Worth more than a book of rules or a score of lectures on behavior was that one challenge to something deep in a boy's remembrance. "Never forget who you are." Wise teachers and parents have always known that the strongest defense the soul has is a determined estimate of ourselves that won't let us fail. We must not hold cheaply either ourselves or the image we carry in our souls.

What was it that kept Joseph down in Egypt, far from home, tempted so terribly there to desert his better self? It seemed that everything was to be gained by sinning, and everything lost by keeping true. But something deep inside of him whispered, and he said, "How can I do this thing and sin against my God?" Joseph knew who he was, and knowing that, he knew that some things were definitely beneath him.

What was it that kept Lincoln through those terrible years of Civil War, when nobody seemed to know what to do, when he carried the weight of the terrible choices in his own great heart? Carl Sandburg, a devoted student of Lincoln, was called to give the commencement address to a graduating class at Harvard. It was at an hour when another war was shaping up and young college men were confused, baffled, and some of them bitter. In his quiet, mystic way, Sandburg said, "Young gentlemen, I think you need the spirit of prayer and humility of Abraham Lincoln who, in 'the divided house' of his day, knew what to do because he knew who he was." There is something there to ponder: a man who knows who he is will know what to do; the whisper in his soul won't let him give in or run away.

What has kept the Jewish people through centuries of stormy history, beaten, persecuted, scattered, but, like Daniel in Babylon, with their faces stubbornly turned toward Jerusalem? A tyrant king there complained about his Jewish slaves. "These stubborn Jews," he said, "do not make good slaves. Something in their stupid religion gives them an air of haughtiness and unfits them for subjection." Exactly! Something in their stupid religion! You can never enslave people who know who they are. You may capture their bodies, but you cannot capture their minds and souls. A man named Moses said, "God made man in his image"—and the Jews have never made good slaves. Only when men forget who they are do they become candidates for servitude. It is in the hearts of cowed people that tyrants raise their thrones. It makes an enormous difference what we think of ourselves, when we remember who we are, and who our neighbor is.

Here, then, is the wider meaning of the great parable of the prodigal. Against this larger background we begin to understand its universal meaning and to see why Jesus told the story to illustrate His mission, what He had come to do in this "far country" which is the world. A boy left home, got lost, landed in swineland among the animals. And then, on a wonderful day, he remembered who he was; he came to himself and said, "What is the son of my father doing here?" It is the New Testament and all Christian history in a single glance. "The Son of man," said Jesus, "is come to seek and to save the lost ones."

The Gnostics had a legend about the lovely Helen of Troy. In one of the wars fought over her beauty she had been left behind in the city of the enemy, and there she lost her mind. She forgot who she was and all that she had been. She sank lower and lower until she was a slave woman in the streets of Tyre. Beautiful Helen had come to that—a thing of shame, shuffling about the streets of that vile seaport, a goddess of sailors. And there, after long search, Menelaus found her, recognized her by a familiar turn of her head, and gently tried to call her back to sanity. Slowly her poor, darkened brain began to clear—a word here, a name there, whispered out of her past. Little by little, the cloud lifted from her memory; into her wonderful eyes came back light and remembrance, until Menelaus took her home, her own beautiful self again.

It is no accident that the world has called Christ "The Saviour." "We must never forget," they said, "that he rescued us from the power of darkness and re-established us in the kingdom of light" (Colossians 1:13, translation by J. B. Phillips).

There He was, out on all the roads where men had lost themselves, among publicans, peasants, and poor folk, among common people who had almost forgotten what it means to be human: not condemning their perversities but talking about their possibilities, telling them who they were and how important they were in the eyes of God. "Even the hairs of your head are numbered, so mindful is He." "Not a star that falls escapes His notice." "Are ye not much better than they?" And if any one of them got lost, He would search His planet cottage with unwearying patience till He found the lost one. They stood out on the edge of the crowds listening, and as they listened something still noble, something not quite dead, stirred within them; these were the whispers of a higher heredity. And out of them, out of the common people, He made His Church.

The impact of Christ upon a few scores of people has changed the world. Presently something began happening in the back streets of the cities that ultimately shook the mighty Roman Empire. Common people began thinking about themselves in higher terms. Slaves and poor folk lifted up their heads with a new sense of dignity. Everyone was important, everyone. They began to think in higher terms of other people. Because Jesus' hand had been on a leper's head a new outflow of charity started—hospitals, care of the sick. Because He had set a child in their midst, all children were vested with a new respect. The old custom in Rome of throwing unwanted babies into the sewers slowed down, stopped. Every person was a somebody. He might be poor, he might be ignorant, the divine image in him might be sadly marred; but every person, the last, the least, and the lost, was an immortal soul for whom Christ had died.

With that vision Christ taught the ancient world to hope. And you can put it down:

If there is to be dignity in the world, we must hold this vision in our hearts, hold it against all enemies without and within ourselves, contend for it on all the roads where people still forget who they are and get lost in far countries of doubt and disillusionment.

# HORNS AND HALOS IN HUMAN NATURE

*And when he came to himself . . .*
LUKE 15:17.

IN THE GREAT parable there is one striking sentence that gives meaning to all the rest of it: ". . . he came to himself." Do not pass lightly over that. Volumes of books could be written on it, and are. This is Jesus' judgment of human nature. The prodigal was not himself in what he was doing, not his real self, his whole self. He was expressing only a part of his nature, the worst part; and it was not until he made up his mind to go home and be a son that he really came to himself, the self for which he was born.

That is important. It is not merely a charitable speech about the prodigal's escapades. Wrapped up in that little sentence is the Christian view of human nature. You see it all through the New Testament. It is based on a revelation made far back in the Old Testament, that God formed man of the dust of the ground, and breathed into his nostrils, and he became a living soul. There is human nature—dust, deity, frailty, dignity—with an original grandeur written into him that will never let him be at rest until he rises to it and comes

56

to himself—to the self for which he was created. That is the Christian interpretation of human nature. Is it true? It is being challenged today by the whole secular world.

There are many reasons for believing that the next great field of research will have to be in the realm of personality, the study of human nature. Man has explored almost everything in the universe except the explorer. We know more about the mysterious forces about us than we know about the mysterious forces within us. We have learned more about the atom than we have learned about the human heart.

A London newspaper carried a cartoon entitled "The Little Thing That Puzzles Him." The scene was a spacious library with stacks of books piled on shelves and lying in confusion on the floor. In the center of the picture was a mirror. In front of the mirror is a man; on his back is written the one word, "Science." The cartoonist is telling us that man is an ingenious creature who has sent his restless mind out into every avenue of life to gather knowledge and compile it in these books. Many of his questions have been answered. Yet as he sits here among his books looking into a mirror, he finds what still remains to him the most intricate and persistent puzzle himself.

What is man? That is one of the great questions back of all the questions. When is man most man? When is he himself? What is the real nature of human nature? Is it good or bad—horns or halos? Is it fixed or flexible, final or changeable? What are the facts about human nature? You can get all sorts of answers to that question. I propose that we keep our Bibles a little longer because, outside of the Bible, I do not know where you will turn to find an honest reading of the facts about human nature.

Suppose we start with what we know. That is a good place to start anything—not out of books, but out of life. Just close the books for a moment. What do we actually know about human nature? A father had just punished his little boy; towering over the youngster, he demanded, "Now will you be a good boy?" The little fellow looked his father straight in the eye and said, "Yes, and no." We all understand that, because that is how it is with us; we are not all horns, not all halos, but a mixture—yes and no, and a conflict between the two. We need no theology to tell us about it. From our own experience we know all about these dark, unmanageable elements in us that we cannot explain. We know how unexpected ugly feelings and unholy thoughts gush up from the unconscious depths of our nature. For no explainable reason, we are cross, peevish, and downright mean. "I was not myself," we say, or "Something got into me." Or "I don't know what got into me."

Up in a New England town lived a prominent business man who, plagued with grouchiness, built a small house on his lawn. He called it his "grouch house." When he felt a bad mood coming on, he shut himself up in his grouch house until the temper was over and he came to himself again.

In the Chinese language there is a character for "peace." It is a house roof with one woman under it. The character for "strife, discord, contention" is the same roof with two women under it. Well, how many women are under your hat, sometimes? And how many men are in every man? We are reasonable today, petulant tomorrow; generous this week, stingy the next; sometimes we are going through all these conflicting moods in one day. One of the great philosophers said, "Really, I'm a decent, kindly, lovable soul, but there is another horrid fellow with repulsive ways who sometimes gets into my clothing, uses my name and gets mistaken for me."

Now, of course, some of you would not admit this for the

world. No horns on you, all halos! How wonderful! We are trying to get an honest reading of the facts about human nature in ourselves. And here they are: dust and deity—a mixture, an everlasting conflict between the halos and the horns.

Certainly we see it in our neighbors. They are a mixture too, with horns showing in the best of them and halos in the worst. There is a bit of the coward in the bravest man and a bit of the hero in the meanest. A bad man looks like a good man sometimes—when his baby is sick, for instance; and a good man looks like a bad man when someone takes his parking space. There is always something in our enemy that we admire, and something in our closest friends that we don't admire. And there is a heap of truth in the old saying:

> There's so much good in the worst of us,
> And so much bad in the best of us,
> That it doesn't behoove any of us
> To find fault with the rest of us.

That is human nature as we actually know it, in ourselves and in our neighbors. And that is what we find in the Bible. Nowhere is the story more vividly told than in this great Book of Life. From Adam on, it is the story of magnificent devotion and shameful degradation. There are all men back there rubbing their foreheads against the stars one day, and trailing glory in the dust the next. David, who made hymns for all the world to sing, didn't always live as he sang. Solomon, who wrote proverbs of wisdom, often chose folly for his bedfellow. My friend Dr. Peter King, from whom I have learned much, first pointed out to me these contrasts in the Bible: "the earthly and the heavenly," "the flesh and the spirit," "the old man and the new," "the first Adam and the second Adam," "the law of sin and the law of Christ," "the beast and the lamb," "Babylon and the New Jerusalem."

59

These are merely terms to state the great reality—that everlasting warfare in man between the halos and the horns.

You see it in literature. Shakespeare put it down in two
great speeches. In "Hamlet" he sees the halos: "What a piece of
work is man, how noble in reason, in action how like an angel,
in apprehension how like a god." Then something happened
to Shakespeare, between "Hamlet" and "King Lear." In
"King Lear" he rubs against the horns: "Man is false of spirit,
bloody of hand; a fox in stealth, a wolf in greediness, a lion in
prey." All literature, poetry, fiction, history, is a continuing
sermon on these two basic texts. They are both true, in different men and in a measure in the same man. Whichever way
you look, this is the true story.

Human nature can be wonderful! Human nature can be
terrible! Nothing it touches is wholly good, and nothing it
touches is wholly evil. You look at it on some days, in some
people, and you see it rise to heights of unbelievable greatness. You see human nature expressed in some ways that
make you proud to belong to such a breed, who for all their
pettiness and littleness have the capacity in them for something noble that rises at times to sheer God-likeness, and
you want to stand up and cheer. You look at it on other days
and in other people, and it is positively hideous. "Man," said
Pascal, "is an incomprehensible monster." You see human
nature lie and cheat and kill—for a bit of land, a bit of
power, a bit of love. You see it crawl like a snake in the grass,
treacherous, brutal, repulsive, drunken and cruel; you want
to put your foot on the thing and stamp it into the earth.
You wonder how in the world God can possibly put up with
it, and you say, "The more I see of people, the more I like
my dog."

At the close of his novel, *Blood and Sand*, Blasco Ibáñez
described a bull fight in which the bull, after being goaded

into madness, turns and catches the matador on his horns, flings him in the air and gores him into bloody insensibility. As the dying matador is carried from the arena, an unearthly roar goes up from the crowd, and the author says, "So we listened to the roar of the only beast there is—humanity." The only beast there is!

Here then, are the facts about human nature; like them or not, they are facts. They are written in history, they are taught in the Bible, they are confirmed in all the experience of man. Not all horns, not all halos—a mixture and a conflict! How stupid we are to ignore the facts, to deny the facts, or to twist the facts to suit a theory! Whatever you are building, you had better build on the facts, whether it is a bridge or a bank or a theology or a society. If you try to build without regard to the facts, the thing will surely come tumbling down. That is exactly what has happened on a large scale in our secular civilization. We have not faced the facts about human nature. We have been sentimental and emotional about human nature. We have alternated between the heights and the depths, between shallow optimism and the deep pessimism of despair.

And that gets us into something that is historically relevant. We know that this Western civilization of ours grew up out of the impulse of two great movements in European life— the Reformation and the Renaissance. Both were revolts against the Medieval Roman Church. Both were attempts to free the soul of man. The Reformation was a spiritual movement in the Church, concerned about moral and spiritual freedom. The Renaissance, on the other hand, although beginning in the Church, came under Greek influence and developed into a secular, humanist movement outside the Church, striking out for the freeing of man's mind. Now, while these two great movements coming along side by side

61

have much in common, and often crossed each other, yet
they took two exactly opposite views of human nature. The
Reformation went too far in pessimism. It concentrated on
the wickedness in life, on the horns in human nature. While
it was right in the conviction that man is sinful in his nature,
and without the grace of God utterly doomed and lost, yet
in its efforts to make that convincing and to show that man
was a sinner in need of regeneration it went beyond the
facts and developed a lopsided character that was anything
but good.

The result was an extreme Calvinism, the teaching of total
depravity of human nature, and "infant damnation"—that
monstrous idea that grew up in the Roman Church in the
dark ages. So depraved was human nature, they said, that
babies were born in this world damned and cursed; and if
they died in infancy without baptism they would roast in
hell forever. Well, that is putting too much emphasis
on the horns. Built on a twisted truth, the Reformation
theology has tended to make a divided and misshapen
Church; it has postponed redemption to beyond the skies; by
teaching man that he must abandon this old world of horns
as a hopeless job and concentrate his efforts on getting his
soul prepared for the world to come it has paralyzed social
reformation, divorced religion from life, bleached out whole
areas of the Gospel and left that outer world without an
ethic. We are suffering still from that distorted and extremely
pessimistic view.

The Renaissance, on the other hand, went too far in
optimism. It forgot all about the horns. Human nature, it
said, was good. Its only fault was its imperfection, its ignorance, its immaturity. Just let man's mind be free, they said;
just let his creative ingenuity start. Out of that came the
easy optimism of the 19th century and the idea of automatic

progress—Spencer's philosophy, Rousseau's "rights of man,"
and "the orginal goodness of human nature." Perhaps the
most optimistic book ever written was published on the eve
of the French Revolution by a French humanist Condorcet.
It was called A Sketch of the Progress of the Human Spirit.
He is described as a man with a genial, enthusiastic disposition. He was carried away by the utopian dream of humanism.
He thought the whole earth would speedily be changed, not
by religion but by reason. It was to be "the age of reason."
He saw the growth of science and democratic ideas. He vi-
sioned the whole world cleansed of crime and poverty and
slavery and war by reason and reason alone. It was a good
book and it has value still, for these are the persistent dreams
of the prophets which history cannot kill. Its fatal fault was
its failure to face the facts about human nature. It failed to
reckon with the horns. Scarcely had his book been published
when he was thrown into prison by the enlightened minds
he had glorified in his book. Next morning he was dead—
killed, some think, by his own hand. And that "age of reason"
became the "age of terror," and hell broke loose on the earth.

The fate of Condorcet is almost a parable of our own
secular age. Reinhold Neibuhr has said, "The errors and
illusions which have made an estimate of our crisis difficult
if not impossible are, almost without exception, various ver-
sions of a single error. They are all expressions of too great
an optimism about the goodness of human nature." Too
great an optimism about the goodness of human nature! We
did not face the facts about human nature. We thought we
had outgrown the horns. We thought all the monsters were
dead. We thought we were civilized. We too were optimistic,
carried away by the utopian dream. "Let's set man's mind
free," we said. "Give him schools, give him a voice in his

63

government, and he'll be all right." That's all we knew about human nature.

That is why we Christians keep saying, to the point of weariness, that, as a matter of life and death, Western man with all his fine ideals, his social conscience and his multitude of books must rediscover the great Book that he has let slip so carelessly out of his hands. He must find the truth again. He must face the facts again. He must make his way back through all the maze of false ideas that have betrayed him to the message of redemption in the New Testament he has scorned. This Book has the truth about life. This Book has no illusions about human nature. Nowhere does it blink the black tragedy of sin. It is the most hopeful Book ever written about man, but nowhere does it cover up the horns. It looks down into the very depths of our being and tells us frankly what we are. "There is none righteous, no, not one." "All have sinned and come short of the glory of God." "If we say we have no sin, we deceive ourselves, and the truth is not in us." That is what we've been doing—deceiving ourselves, trying to make life go apart from the Father; we have built a civilization on the idea that there is no sin anywhere and nothing wrong with anybody except that which can be educated away, or organized away, or legislated away by the pooling of man's wisdom.

Browning said it was the realism of the Bible that won him to Christ. In a time when others talked blithely about "the nothingness of sin" and treated lightly the wrong they knew was in them, he said that the Bible looked him straight in the eye and told him he was a sinner on the path to hell. He took heart in that, because he knew at last he had found "an honest reading of the facts." "God be merciful to me, a sinner." That is realism. "Who shall deliver me from the body of this death?" That is realism. That is a man talking honestly out of his experience. "Thank God through our Lord Jesus Christ." The New Testament is forever trying to get man to see himself, to face the facts about himself, and, by the grace of God and the power of Christ, to "come to himself."

Now, there is one class of people who bring out all the horns on my head and make me forget that, as a preacher, I'm supposed to have a halo or two. I share the wish of some people that we could invent some form of ecclesiastical profanity which we church folk could use, so that a minister could be normal when he hits his thumb, or when he meets some people who ought to get what's coming to them. The people who try my religion more than any other are those who meet every proposal for human betterment or change with a superior smile and the old statement, "You can't change human nature."

Someone said, "There's more downright blasphemy in that sentence than in a tent full of top sergeants." There is more downright atheism in that attitude than in all the professed Godlessness of Russia, for at least Russia believes that something can be changed. It is the real denial of God, of His power, His purpose, His mission. It is a denial of the whole New Testament. From "the year 1," people have been saying, "You can't change human nature." That is nothing but a rationalization of defeatism, the refuge of prodigals who won't go home, the resistance of the secular man to the call of God within his soul to get up and be himself, the self for which he was created.

What do you mean—can't change human nature? If you mean by that only that we will always have trouble with the horns, then you are right. We shall always have to struggle with our lower nature, and we glory in the fight. And if you mean that we cannot hope to be rid of the great driving in-

65

stincts with which we were born, you are still right. But who wants to get rid of them? Who wants to get rid of his sex, of the power to produce life, of ambition, of power to shape life, of temper, of the capacity for clean anger? Not even God would take these away from us, for they are our native equipment; they are the qualities that make us men.

But if you mean what most people mean, that sin is natural, that human nature is synonymous with being weak or wicked, that it is fixed and final and that nothing can be done to change it, then, thank God, it is a lie. For the whole mission of Christ, the whole assumption of the Gospel, is that there is a power that can and does change human life. Christ came to bring man to himself, to restore man to Sonship. "To as many as received him, to them gave he power to become the sons of God."

Read through the New Testament and close the Book and see if you can still say, "You can't change human nature." Or study the history of the Anglo-Saxon race coming up from savagery by the power of the Cross and see if you can still say, "You can't change human nature." "Such were some of you," said Paul, "drunkards, idolators, thieves, sorcerers. But you are changed, you are made over, you are new persons in Christ."

We do not need a new faith for the Western world. We need new insights and a new grasp for the faith we already hold. Our pessimism today is unjustified. We sometimes behave as if God were dead, and as if Christ had never come.

Jesus never despaired of human nature. He never lost faith in the common people. He knew more about human nature than anyone else ever knew, but He never lost His faith in men—not even at the Cross where He was beaten back into the dark by the same brand of brutality that is making cynics now. "Father, forgive them, for they know not what they do. They are ignorant. They are not themselves."

So, when I get the blues about human nature and when I am tempted to lose faith in people or in the future, I turn to Christ. He keeps me believing in common people. He keeps me believing in the future. More than that, he keeps me believing in myself.

91-94.

*Excellent* ✓

# HOW FREE IS FREEDOM?

*Father, I have sinned against heaven, and before thee, and am
no more worthy to be called thy son: make me as one of thy
hired servants.* LUKE 15:18-19.

THAT WAS THE little speech the prodigal son memorized and
mumbled as he trudged homeward in his rags from the far
country of disillusionment. "Make me a hired man!" He had
run into a mystery, and into the awesome moment of realization when freedom, in some strange way, ceases to be free
and becomes bondage. Turning it over in his tortured mind,
he found words to speak his degradation—"Make me a hired
man." He had made such a sorry mess of his liberty. He was
now ready to trade it off for security, a job, a place to sleep
and a bit of bread. "Make me a hired man. I am not good
enough to be a son."

I wonder if you see the full force of that. Whole areas of
humanity today are trading liberty for security, and losing
both. Why? If we knew the answer to that we would understand better the true nature of secularism, and of how deeply
life without God is corroding the spirit of men and making
them less than human. Little by little, over the past quarter
of a century, we have watched the passion for freedom burn
low; people in one country after another surrender liberty

to some collective authority until, as the late General Smuts said, "In the old world, which was the cradle of European civilization, the great principles are cast aside as a worn-out garment; even the desire for freedom is gone." Why?

The most popular diagnosis is that freedom has proven too difficult. It is interpreted as a failure of nerve, a decadence of the spirit, a weakening of the will to be free. "Men are slaves," said Berdyaev, "because freedom is difficult and slavery is easy." There is much to be said for that point of view. History is full of illustrations of people sinking into servitude because they wouldn't face the hard fight to stay free. Someone asked a tramp how he decided directions and made up his mind where he wanted to go. The tramp said that was no problem. When he woke up in the morning, he looked to see which way the wind was blowing and he went along with it. That is what made him a tramp; he went along with the wind, which was the way of least resistance.

It is what makes history disheartening too. You get the feel of it in Exodus, where Moses is trying to get his people out of slavery in Egypt. Their long years of servitude had corroded their spirit, bleached all the fight out of them. Every time they confronted a hard problem, they grumbled against Moses and begged to go back. "Let us alone," they said, "that we may serve the Egyptians. Better a slave in Egypt than a corpse in the wilderness." They had lost the will to fight and struggle against the wind. It seemed easier to sell their wretched bodies for bread and soup than to face the hard struggle of the road.

That was the lure of Fascism. Hitler came to people who felt themselves hopeless against the winds of fate. He promised them food, security, the loot of empire, if they would surrender to him their souls, the right to think and venture, and all that made men human. It is the perpetual lure of the

69

totalitarian dream. To the little man who can't face the wind, this mechanized world seems too vast, too complicated, the struggle too difficult to make. He can lessen his struggle by reducing his freedom, by letting other people think for him. Just give him a bit of bread. Just make him a hired man. We have watched it happen across the world—men and women in a mood of fatigue and frustration, attaching themselves to the strong man who promised bread and protection. They were willing to surrender their rights as sons of the Father, to throw themselves at the mercy of the mass will, and that took them straight to tyranny. "Make me a hired man. It is too hard to be a son."

But we are convinced that this interpretation is not the whole story. I propose that we come at it from another angle, less conducive to pride and smugness on our part. There are millions of people in the world for whom freedom has lost its enchantment. They don't want it, not because it is too difficult, but because it has been held too lightly, because the people who have had it and prided themselves in it have misused it. Like the boy of the parable, they have hurt themselves in the abuse of it. "We have used our freedom in such a way," says John Foster Dulles, "that it seems a dangerous concept to those who have never had it, to whom it has been nothing but a word." They are not impressed with our freedom. They don't want it. They are ready to trade it off for something that gives more stability to life. Here in the land of the free, this is really something for us to think about—the awful misuse of liberty which has put famine in the hearts of men and disillusioned them even of their great ideals.

Here we have hold of something big. Liberty is a tremendous thing, too big to talk about; it is one of the great words of human speech, and nobody can define it. Whole libraries have been written around it, but nobody can say what it means. That is because it is so intensely spiritual. It has its roots in our spiritual nature; it didn't come out of an Act of Congress but out of the unfathomable mystery of life itself; it is one of the inalienable rights which we possess as the potential sons of God. It is when we forget this, when we forget its spiritual nature, when we make it an end in itself, when we divorce it from other great endowments and try to make it stand alone, that our trouble with freedom begins. We could paraphrase Jesus' words: "Man cannot live by freedom alone, but by every word that comes from the mouth of God." If men are disillusioned about freedom, it is not freedom that has failed us but false freedom, freedom divorced from the other great words of God. That is what I want to ask: "How free is freedom?" Every attempt to find freedom at the expense of other compelling ideals leads to famine, futility, and disillusionment. "Make me a hired man."

Let us start with the attempt to find liberty apart from community. A certain man bought lumber to build a small tool house on his lot; he was notified by a city official that fire regulations would not permit him to build a wooden structure there. He said it was his own lot; he'd build what he wanted. Finally, of course, he had to give in, and he changed to brick. He was informed at the City Hall that before he could build anything, he must have a permit. That made him angry. A permit! He would buy no permit; he showed his contempt by spitting on the sidewalk. For that he was arrested, and paid a fine. Thoroughly angered now, he drove off from the City Hall in a huff, ran through a traffic light and again was arrested. He paid his fine, swearing that he would not live in such a town. When he reached the city limits, he was halted by a health inspector. "You can't leave this town; it has been quarantined for smallpox!"

Probably it is only a story; yet, conceivably, it could be

true. "How free is freedom?" There is no such thing as absolute freedom. Why pretend that there is? The stars don't have it; they are hemmed in by the law. The ocean doesn't have it; it is hemmed in by law. Man doesn't have it; he is hemmed in by other men who make up the solidarity of life. How free is any man in a modern city? Only as free as the rights of his neighbor will permit him to be. There was a time when we didn't have to worry much about our neighbor. In the era of wide-open spaces in America the frontiersman was free. He was an individualist, like Robinson Crusoe on his island before he saw the footprint. When he decided to build a house, he put it where he wanted it. He consulted only his own interest and convenience about the house he wanted, about the kind of roof to put on it, about where to keep his cows and chickens, and how to dispose of the garbage, and about when and where to hunt and fish. There were no licenses to obtain, no traffic laws to interrupt his course. He was the rugged individualist who could sing with some measure of reality, "Don't fence me in!"

But the frontier has passed. Our neighbors have arrived. A powerful new reality has been born in the earth with the coming of the great machine. The community of man has reached out and hemmed him in, and rugged individualism has run headlong into something more rugged than itself— into a complicated, interrelated world community in which every man is linked up with every other man. Most people have not learned yet how rugged that reality is, how deeply it has challenged our traditional notions of liberty. I read somewhere that after a famous novelist died, they found among his papers a list of suggested story plots, ideas for possible future stories, of which he had underscored this one: "A widely separated family inherits a house in which they have to live together." Too bad that someone can't write a

72

story on that, and tell us how to do it, for it is the great new problem of mankind! We have inherited a house, a great "world-house" in which we have to live together—Gentiles and Jews, black and white, strong and weak, a family widely separated in ideas, culture, interests—who, because we can never again live without each other, must learn, somehow, in one world, to live together. It is useless to rebel against this reality or to pretend it isn't here. The great community is here. The mechanical genius of man has made it. The gregarious instinct has produced it. There has never been anything like it in history. Back of it, many of us believe, is the mighty power of God working out His purpose, pushing us into one big house where every man is linked with every other man and where individualism in the old sense is not only immoral but impossible.

That is why all our notions about liberty are in a welter of confusion. Little wonder we are mixed up! Listen to the debate in high and low places, focused at the point where the lines of individual freedom and social responsibility meet, and see what a fog we are in. The smug assumption that it is a simple choice between right and left, and that the only threat to freedom we need to be disturbed about comes from the Communist and the thousand-and-one brands of collectivism is a dangerous misreading of the facts. Plenty of people are saying that, beating the tom-toms for a Holy Crusade against the Communists and Socialists, with the naïve assumption that all we have to do to keep our freedom is to get back to the old-fashioned American individualism. How are we going to get back to it? And if we got back, what would we have?

Let me quote Dr. Walter Marshall Horton on that: "It may be well that we are called to leadership in the conflict between Christianity and the 'totalitarian state,' but our warfare would

73

be less bigoted and more Christian if we realized that individualism of the American type represents as great a variation in one direction from the Christian norm as totalitarianism is in the opposite direction."

Our choice is not a simple one between individualism and collectivism, but a choice between them and a concept higher than both. We reject Communism and Socialism because they exalt the state community by destruction of liberty. We reject individualism because it exalts liberty at the expense of community.

We must re-examine our concept of liberty in the light of its Christian rootage. "You are called to liberty," said Peter, "only use not your liberty as an occasion of the flesh, but through love be servants of one another." That is the note missing in the secular debate—liberty that loves and serves the community.

That is why I can't get excited about the conflict between right and left. Morally, there is little difference between them. Someone said that a Leftist is one who wants two dollars more a day and a Rightist is one who wants a hundred thousand dollars more a year. What is the difference? Liberty is our big word, and we must make the hard fight to stay free, but let's be sure it is liberty we get. The trouble is that somewhere along the line this great idea got itself lifted out of its Christian rootage, got confused with *laissez faire*—that quaint idea of Adam Smith's, that if we follow our own self-interests, the course will, somehow, automatically work out for the interests of the whole. Do you suppose Christianity can make peace with that? Christianity is almost as much in conflict with that irresponsible freedom—that "every-man-for-himself" notion of it—as it is with totalitarianism itself. The only liberty worth keeping, or that any people can keep, is the Christian liberty that seeks not its own, but loves and serves the community.

74

Let us go on to another phase of it: the attempt to find freedom at the expense of conscience. Here is this unforgettable story of a boy coming back from the pig trough, retold in tragic repetition in the lives of millions ever since—the story of freedom without conscience and a famine at the end of it. You see, he took his freedom and used it to enslave himself. He walked down the road one sunny morning, his young blood singing "Don't fence me in," and lived his days in the exuberant hilarity of a soul set free. No one to tell him what to do, when to come in at night, how to spend his money; there were no rules to suppress his gaiety, there was no stuffy religion to interfere with his rights. With a toss of his head he left them all behind—parental discipline, moral restraint, religious responsibility. Just a toss of his head and he was free.

But it wasn't that simple, after all, as shortly he came to see. "He came to himself," the parable says. He came to that other part of his self with which he thought he was finished.

Funny thing about conscience; we are not supposed to have one you know. One psychologist said that conscience was a primitive left-over, like the vermiform appendix, which the doctor cuts out because we don't need it any more. Yet it seems to tag along, if only as a "still, small voice." The prodigal couldn't get away from his conscience. These rights of his were not paying out as they had promised. The more he got what he wanted, the less he wanted what he got. And one day he ran smack into the truth of it: He saw that freedom isn't merely a matter of *rights*, but also a matter of *right*. To indulge your rights at the expense of right, or to act on your rights as though right had no existence at all, is not liberty. It is just another kind of tyranny.

"No bad man," said Epictetus, "is really free. We shall have to examine our freedom again in the light of this. For a long time we have been talking about our rights, pulling freedom up

75

out of its ethical rootage until it has come to mean for millions little more than the right to do what they want. Right is not even considered; right is only relative anyway, a lot of stuffy opinions handed down as a matter of custom and convenience. This is a free country; everybody decides for himself what is right. So with a toss of the head we dismiss right and go off singing—"Don't fence me in."

Nothing but famine comes out of it. Divorce rates go higher. The crime bill goes higher. You get a good picture in modern fiction. Pick up almost any novel and there is the story— free people misusing freedom, getting into some kind of pig trough. Aldous Huxley's story, *Eyeless in Gaza*, for example, is a story of wealthy people educated, and emancipated from all the old taboos but pathetically empty and with no capacity for loyalty to anything. They talk continually of their right to be happy, of their right to be free, yet they haven't the first idea why they were *meant* to be free. They go to the seashore, rush off to the Riviera, drink themselves full, sit around tables and play themselves empty trying frantically to get away from the emptiness of others, and never getting away from their own empty little selves. How free is freedom? It is never free enough to break away from conscience. You can have all the liberties and yet not be free. Jesus said that to His people, "You shall know the truth and the truth shall make you free." They said, "Who? Us? Evidently you don't know whom you are talking to. We are the people, the free people. We are Abraham's children. We have never been slaves to anyone." And Jesus put it plainly, "People who sin, who do not follow truth and righteousness, are always slaves. Only those who follow truth and right are really free." Jesus Himself lived under a dictator. And yet, He was freer than Pilate or any of his conquerors.

> Our fathers, chained in prisons dark,
> Were still in heart and conscience free.

Freedom is of the spirit. Only those who follow truth are really free.

There is also an attempt to find freedom apart from its challenge, and this is the positive side of it. Someone says that the best way to show that a stick is crooked is not to spend time arguing about the crookedness but just to put a straight stick alongside it. What is freedom for? Why do we want it? That is the basic question. After all, there is no particular virtue in wanting freedom for itself. Any bird can match that. Even a fish wants to be free. Every wild animal will fight to the death for its freedom. Why do you want freedom? What is it for? That is the straight stick to lay down alongside the crookedness.

Freedom may be the emptiest of all words if it means only absence from restraint, or absence of authority. "Freedom of speech," says Dr. Robert M. Hutchins, "is empty unless we have something to say." What good is free speech if we use it to lie and fill the air with bunk? Freedom of worship is empty if we have no God to worship. Someone said that some of our people here in the land of the free were terribly upset when Russia closed its churches, but didn't even know that their own American churches were open! Freedom of religion? —They were free of it entirely. Freedom from kings, tyrants, autocratic authority?—Of what use is all that if we take it as the inalienable right to do as we please? The Prodigal son had that, and it took him straight to a pig trough. Somewhere Dr. Buttrick pointed out that the Emperor Nero had all four freedoms, and he used them all to make himself a scoundrel.

Freedom is no good if you make it an end in itself and divorce it from Divine purpose. "You shall know the truth, and the truth shall make you free." That is positive. Not freedom from something, but freedom to something. Not absence of restraint, but presence of possibility. Not just the power to do as we want, but the power to do what God wants. There is a vast difference between Christian liberty and the cheap substitute secularism has made of it. When Moses stood before Pharaoh saying, "Let my people go," his dream of liberty was no cheap notion of release from restraint and authority; he wanted his people free that they might serve the will of God and be the sons of God. No sooner had he released them from the authority of Pharaoh than he confronted them with another, the authority of the Ten Commandments and the authority of God, and bound them to a higher King.

When Martin Luther struck out for religious freedom, he had no interest in freeing men to do as they liked; he wanted them free to respond to the call of God. When Jesus preached His first sermon, He said He had come to set the captives free. Yet the first step He made in the process was to bind them to Himself: "Follow me." That is the great paradox of freedom. You are never really free until you are bound, voluntarily mastered by something greater than yourself; you are never free in music until you are bound to it; you are never free in painting a picture, or preaching a sermon, or living a life, until in heart and soul and spirit you are bound to it. "Make me a captive, Lord, and then I shall be free."

Bob Bartlett, that irrepressible explorer, said that on a voyage one summer he and his party brought back a large number of caged birds. Along about mid-ocean one restless bird escaped from his cage. In ecstasy of freedom, he flew away and they watched him out across the water until he disappeared in the blue of the sky. They said, "That bird is lost." But after some hours had passed, to their surprise, they saw him again coming toward the ship on heavy wing. Panting and breathless,

78

the little feathered prodigal dropped upon the deck. Far over the trackless water, how eagerly he had sought that ship again! It was no longer a prison but a home and the only way across the deep.

There is no liberty except in the will of God. Every other freedom is an illusion. We batter and bruise ourselves in vain attempts to get away from God, but to find at last that He is the only way across. And every excursion into the far countries of false freedom brings us back, at last, to this:

Make me a captive, Lord, and then I shall be free.

For if the Son shall make you free, you shall be free indeed.

See 91-92 etc

Excellent

# WHAT THE DICKENS IS SIN?

*Father, I have sinned . . .*
LUKE 15:21.

How LONG IS it since you heard a sermon on sin? A year, two years, five? For quite some time the subject of sin has been almost taboo as sermon material. We have been told that people are too much and too morbidly concerned with sin. It is not mentally healthy to fasten our thoughts on our failures. It is depressing to dwell on our faults. What is needed is a positive, wholesome outlook on life. If we must have a religion, let us have a cheerful religion and quit moaning *misereres* in the church. Let's all live on the sunny side of the street.

None of us wants to be morbid or gloomy or dwell on the negative side of anything. We are quite aware that churchmen have called some things sin which are not sin, and that theologians, in emphasizing the evils in human nature, have sometimes exaggerated and distorted the true picture. We agree that we should follow the positive, New Testament emphasis on the divine possibilities in man rather than the negative, Augustinian emphasis on the depravity of man. Nevertheless, here is the world we live in, and "restless is the heart." We are in for a rude awakening if, reacting against the exaggeration, we get lopsided in another direction and ignore or modify

80

the tragic reality of sin. If the idea of sin has faded out in the modern man's mind it does not necessarily mean he is getting too intelligent to accept it. It may mean that he is getting too morally insensitive to discern it. Martineau said, "Sin is the only thing in the universe of which it may be truly said, 'The more you practice it, the less you know its nature.'"

So, at the risk of seeming negative, I ask you to look again at the New Testament insight on sin against the background of the parable of the prodigal son.

It was a college girl who asked, "Professor, what the dickens is sin?" It is a legitimate question, however it may be phrased; and it deserves a more solid answer than it usually gets in the delightful little books that explain it so cheerfully away. Why is it that almost every amateur feels quite qualified to speak on religion? That is not true in other fields. It is generally assumed in the educational world that no one has the right to teach mathematics or biology unless he knows something about the subject. Yet on the matter of religion almost anyone can speak with authority. If one has made a million dollars, become a tennis champion, or written a best-seller novel he is thereby made competent to advance snappy pronouncements on God and the human soul. We tip our hat to Miss Ruth Roman. "Actresses," she said, "are always being asked to give their advice on dozens of subjects. I have worked pretty hard learning how to do my job, but that certainly hasn't qualified me to give advice on love, fashions, or how to bake beans."

Every generation produces a horde of quack doctors in the realm of spiritual things who, unhampered by any knowledge of the facts, spin fascinating theories about "the nothingness of evil." That is the phrase. I have lifted it out of an essay. We should try to get the facts. We have a right to expect in this field the same careful analysis, the same respect for fact, the same patient examination of realities that the scientist must make in his field. I mean that we should pay some attention to men who have made a study of the human soul—men like William James, for example, or men who have vitally experienced religion, like the writers of the New Testament. I think this is a fair way to get at it. Ask these questions: What do the New Testament writers say? And do the facts as we know them correspond to their insights?

When you read the New Testament you will find no explanation of the origin of evil. The New Testament writers assume its existence as they assume their own. Sin is a moral twist in human life, they say; it is something which ought not to be, a downward bent in human nature that disorganizes life, contaminates the springs of action and sets up discord in the world. It is not merely violation of some taboo, but rebellion against the Law of God within the mind. Furthermore, they recognize it as an hereditary fact, passed on and perpetuated from generation to generation, going clear back to the first conscious life and, therefore, as universal as life itself. "All men," they say, "have sinned. If any man says he has not sinned, he lies; he deceives himself and the truth is not in him." They never tone it down. They never soften it with extenuating words. They do not call it "mistake" or "blunder" or "goodness in the making" or "absence of light." They call it "sin"—something of which every last individual on earth is guilty, and from which every last individual must be saved; or, refusing the saving grace of God, be lost.

Now, it does not matter whether that view is optimistic or popular or modern. The question is, Is it true? What are the facts? It is better, said Henry Van Dyke, to be sobered by the saddest fact than to be deluded by the merriest lie. What are the facts, and how do we get at them?

Suppose we look at the world; suppose we forget sermons and preachers and priests and gloomy theologians as if they had never been; suppose we try to look at human life as we actually know it to be. Let's take a walk down the street. What do the facts we find there teach us? On what assumption do men habitually act? There are thousands of men out there who have never read the New Testament, and who therefore haven't the foggiest notion of what it teaches about sin. But in their everyday relationships they live and move and have their being on an assumption of its existence.

You ask a banker to loan you money, and right off you start him thinking about the sin question. He may know nothing of the origin of evil, but he knows how to call up the credit department. You take out some life insurance, and the company will have a question or two to ask you at this point. On the street corner you run into a uniformed policeman. Who is he? What is he doing there? He is a silent witness to the reality of sin. Why do you lock your door at night? Why is it that at this very moment the key to your automobile is in your pocket? The makers of automobiles are not theologically trained, but they are theologically conditioned. They may never have read the Book, but they have read human nature and are under no illusions about the facts.

Why is it that when you get a little money you head straight for the bank where, every night, they swing shut a ten-inch steel door on the bank vault, leave a light burning over it, and employ a watchman to see that it is kept burning? Whether or not you believe in theological doctrines, for your own self-protection you are obliged to believe what the New Testament teaches about human nature. It is all very well to talk in sheltered classrooms about the "nothingness of evil," "the absence of light," and Rousseau's "original goodness." They are very lovely theories, but out in the world we cannot act on them. Out there we are realists. Out there we are New

Testament believers; we accept the verdict of the gloomy theologians on the question of human sin.

Uncle Sam has no illusions, either. Count up the cost of G-men, law courts, investigations and investigators, and Congress passing thirteen hundred new laws every year; bring before your mind's eye all the coercive paraphernalia designed to restrain unruly human nature, billions upon billions of dollars worth of it, and it becomes immediately apparent that whatever may be our theory, we agree with the New Testament appraisal of sin far more than we realize. Sin is no ghost that the priests have conjured up, no creation of minds made morbid by the fear of God. Sin is the most realistic fact with which humanity is compelled to deal. When men set up a city government, they have to think of the sin question. When men draw up a constitution for a nation, they have to think of the sin question. Human nature being what it is, they must have checks and balances, protections and restrictions. Sin is real, and every day, whatever may be our fancy theories, we live by that sound assumption.

Now suppose we come closer and look within ourselves. It is an amazing thing, as Dr. Buttrick once said, that we should find ourselves debating the reality of sin, "since the fact of it is axiomatic"—and, we might add, since we all have inside information on the subject.

Dwight L. Moody used to say that the man with whom he had most trouble was the man inside his coat. Every man knows that when he gets himself on the carpet. Paul said, in effect, "When I would do good, evil is present with me. I find in myself a conflict between the law of God and the law of sin." That isn't merely one man's theology; that is testimony, and Paul's honest candor is echoed within the secret heart of every one of us. We need no book to tell us about it. We know when we defy God. We know when we take the

84

lower road instead of the higher. We know when an unclean passion leaves a stain. We know how mixed in motive even our goodness is, how desperately difficult it is to keep the man inside the coat from fouling up the noblest thing we think or do.

Ian Maclaren has a story of Andrew Harris, who was elected elder of the Church. Came the night to hear objections. The moderator called, "Andrew Harris. Is there any reason why he should not be elected as elder in the kirk?" No one arose, for all believed in him. But Andrew Harris himself arose and said, "My friends, there is a man in this city of whom I am deeply envious, and wherefore because I am a true witness against the life of Andrew Harris, I now object and declare he is not fit to be an elder in the kirk." Most of us are not so honest. We would never admit openly to this self in us that wants to strut, to the "I" that wants to be God, to the man inside the coat and the contempt he holds for other people deep down in the hush and hidden places of the heart. We would never come right out and admit it. So we cover up; and wear a false face; we put on, as some animals do, a protective coloration; we try to make the thing seem admirable, even righteous— a deception which is itself a part of the nature of sin. Every man who understands himself and is honest with himself is a true witness against himself at this point.

What the dickens is sin? We know what it is. It is all the things we've done in violation of God's law within the mind. It is more than that. "To him that knoweth to do good and doeth it not, to him it is sin."

> I never cut my neighbor's throat,
>   My neighbor's purse I never stole;
> I never spoiled his house and land,
>   *But God have mercy on my soul!*

85

For I am haunted night and day
By all the deeds I have not done,
That unattempted loveliness,
Oh, costly valor, never won.
GUILTY, by Marguerite Wilkinson.

Dr. Harry Emerson Fosdick preached a sermon on "The Rediscovery of Sin"—an illuminating title. He said, "Today, we and our hopes and all our efforts after goodness are up against a powerful antagonism, something tragic and terrific in human nature that turns our lovliest qualities to evil and our finest endeavors into failure. Our fathers called that sin. If you have a better name for it, use it, but recognize that realistic fact."

Go back and underscore that last sentence; it is the key to the understanding of something fascinating and far-reaching happening in our time. If what our fathers called "sin" seems vague and unreal to our generation, it is not because sin or the sense of it has lessened. It is mostly because we have been calling sin by other names. A new science has been born in our day, a new way of looking at the human soul. With the coming of this new study called "psychology" (which, literally, means "soul study") we have new labels for old evils, a whole new vocabulary for what in former ages we were content to call "sin."

Substitute the word "complex" for the word "sin," "frustration" for what our fathers called "conviction," "neurosis" or "morbid fear" for what in a less enlightened day was called "demon possession," and the old devils are all back, dressed up in raiment and baptized with new names. When this new science first came in (and it is well to remember it is new, and immature, and not yet a century old) it was feared by churchmen as all new things are, and looked upon with considerable suspicion. For here was a study of the soul which, in its early

86

stages and in some of its later developments, seemed to jauntily dispense with God, and even with the soul itself. Isn't it a bit odd that intelligent men devoting their lives to the study of the soul could only conclude that there wasn't any soul at all? The psychiatrists joked about it. They said, "We first lost the soul, then we lost the consciousness, and now, with the coming of behaviorism, we have left nothing but misbehavior."

That first fear, however, has almost wholly disappeared. To be sure, there are psychiatrists who do not believe in God, just as there are surgeons who do not believe in God. Certain schools of psychology are based on a nonreligious, mechanistic foundation. Nevertheless, clinics are springing up in the churches and God is working in the clinics, because the insights of psychology, far from denying the New Testament, have brought enormous light and confirmation to its basic teachings. Go down with Freud into the lower depth which he called "the subconscious," examine with him what goes on in that dark cellar of concealment, and you will get a whiff of depravity of which even John Calvin never dreamed. Far more real than we realize are the penalties, judgments and retributions; these are not waiting for a far-off judgment day, but are going on continually down in the hidden areas of the heart. Every thought and deed is registered there with infallible accuracy; so in every fearful experience from childhood on, and all the heaped-up hereditary instincts coming down through long racial memory. The Freudian calls it "subconscious." Our fathers called it "original sin." It is naïve to think that we have removed it by redefining it.

Today an overwhelming volume of literature is being written fortifying the message of the New Testament about the hidden things of the heart—about the effect of guilt upon personality, the corrosion of resentment, the seeping poison of self-centered living. People who never would have listened to the Word of

God from a church pulpit are having it preached to them now in a psychiatric clinic. And they are being told by soft-spoken men who do not wave their arms and shout, as we preachers do, that what they need to be whole again is to get the buried stuff up out of the dark; to bring it to the surface of the mind, air it, ventilate it, get rid of it! What is new about that? That is precisely what the New Testament teaches! Or *is* it? At this point we have some questions to ask.

Can we deal with sin as soul sickness only, or heal a wounded conscience as a doctor straightens out a twisted bone? Is there something missing in that therapy? What did Dr. Hocking of Harvard mean when he said, "The secular psychiatrist all too often undertakes a work which, purely as a psychiatrist, he cannot finish"? And what did the psalmist mean when he said, "Against thee, and thee only have I sinned"? Against Thee?

The New Testament tells the story of the Cross, and we have made the Cross the symbol of our faith. We do not see sin in its true light until we see it there, set against the background of a divine love that suffered in the sinning. Perhaps a doctor or a psychiatrist can look impersonally upon your sin or mine, but there is a depth psychology even deeper than his probings. Our sin is not only against ourselves, our health, our welfare. It is a sin against Him, against a Father who suffers in our sinning.

Get at it this way. Is a drunken boy staggering and reeling down the street comedy or tragedy? If you are talking about my boy, I can tell you. Love makes the difference in how we measure sin. To look at this mad world through the eyes of a novelist or a newspaper columnist who writes the events as he sees them is one thing. To look at the world through the eyes of one who shares the divine compassion and cares deeply enough to carry the hurt of it is quite another. All around us are the tragedies of life—broken lives, shattered homes, deserting husbands, men dying on battlefields, children orphaned by war and half-orphaned by broken homes. These are the events that make up life.

Novelists write the stories in their books. Newspapers announce a New York scandal in lurid headlines. From a distance it can be viewed quite casually. Or on the moving picture screen it can be worked up into something quite interesting, and even attractive. From a distance, from the standpoint of the spectator, it doesn't seem like sin at all. But let it walk in your door, let the girl in the scandal be your daughter, let the knife stick in your heart, let sin lay hold on someone near and dear to you, and watch him get coarse and crude and cheap! Through the eyes of love and through the eyes of love alone we see sin for what it is.

Do you see what we are saying here? We are getting close to the mightiest truth ever announced on this planet. We get a hint of it in the parable. "There was a boy," Jesus tells us, "who broke with his father and left home." He went on in a few terse phrases to tell a story, such a common story, so familiar, so often repeated, so near to where our hearts live. We can readily fill in the details—the wrong crowd, the wrong dreams, the late hours, the free life. The far country was in the prodigal's mind long before he set out for it. In his home they knew that; they saw it coming; they pleaded with him, and the elder brother censured him. Then, finally, in spite of the pleadings and chance after chance to straighten up, the down-pull was too strong; one day when their patience was exhausted they reluctantly let him go. His room in the father's house was empty, and over the house was the shadow of disgrace.

There were his chums who had grown up with him. "Too

bad," they said. "He was a good fellow. What got ii
Then they proceeded to forget the unpleasant though
were the teachers who taught him in the synagogue, whc
than once, had reported his irreverence for the Law.
bad about young Ben. Strange, too. Good blood, fine fan.
What a pity." And they proceeded to forget, or to rememb
it only as a warning for the younger boys. There was the father's
business partner. "Too bad about that boy. Poor old Eleazar
is all broken up, as good a father as any boy ever had. I feel
awfully sorry for Eleazar." And then, in the press of things,
it joggled out of mind.

But in the boy's home there was the father. Sin had walked
in his door. He went about his work, did what had to be done
and more. He worked too hard, the neighbors said. He kept
discreetly still before the servants, who could not look at him
nor bear to read the sadness in his eyes. And the gray in his
hair grew grayer, and the lines in his face deeper. Friends tried
one day to talk to him, to tell him that, for his own health's
sake, he must not take it so hard. And he said, "Yes, I know.
I know other boys go wrong, some much worse. But to think
that Ben—my Ben . . ." And there you have it.

There it is, all of it—Bethlehem, Calvary, the New Testament, and the call of the Church through the centuries. That
is what makes the difference. You see it through the eyes of
love. The nearer we get to the heart of God, to the heart that
broke, the clearer we see sin for what it is and understand
why there had to be a Cross upon a hill.

If you want the Scripture for it, here it is. I have never yet
been able to preach on it. "God so loved the world . . ."

"God so loved the world that he gave His only begotten
son, that whosoever believeth on him should not perish but
have everlasting life."

# FORGIVE US OUR TRESPASSES

*". . . his father saw him, and had compassion, and ran, and fell on his neck, and kissed him."*     LUKE 15:20.

A TYPICALLY MODERN woman wrote a verse that found its way into the columns of a daily newspaper:

> I wish there were some one
> Who would hear confession.
> Not a priest—I do not want to be told of
>     my sins;
> Not a mother—I do not want to give sorrow;
> Not a friend—she would not know enough;
> Not a lover—he would be too partial;
> Not a God—He is far away;
> But some one who would be friend, lover, mother,
>     priest, God, all in one,
> And a stranger besides—who would not condemn
>     or interfere;
> Who, when everything is said from beginning to
>     end,
> Would show the reason of it all
> And tell you to go ahead
> And work it out your own way.
>
>                     Jeanne D'Orge,
>             in N. Y. *Times Book Review.*

"I have sinned," the prodigal said to his father. "I have sinned." And in the heart of every human there is something

91

that understands him. God has given every human soul a sense of guilt, a vague, uneasy restlessness, and it is one of our most precious possessions. It is the proof of our sonship. It is the call of Eternity. It is God's unbroken hold upon our hearts. What a pity we have gone to the shallows about the meaning of that! At no point has the secular view of life proved more bankrupt than in its incapacity to understand and effectively deal with the reality of human sin. Jauntily it has dismissed sin as irrelevant and turned from the great depths, the profound wisdom of the Hebrew prophets, the realism of Shakespeare and the great dramatists and the message of redemption in the New Testament to the unbelievably shallow philosophy of Rousseau about the goodness of man and his ability to save himself without God.

Meanwhile, the sin of man has piled up in tragic consequence. It has not helped much to call it error, absence of good, false concept of mind—as though, by waving a metaphysical wand, we could banish jails, wars, concentration camps. Something is here, something, filling life with tragic consequence, and if it isn't real it might as well be. Neither has it helped much to call sin by other names, by the soft names that take responsibility out of action. We've had our share of that, too. If you get a broken home, it isn't anything that anybody is responsible for. It is incompatibility, or some other word the lawyer supplies at fifty dollars a dozen.

> In olden days when people heard
> Some swindler huge had come to grief,
> They used a good old Saxon word,
> And called the man a thief;
> But language such as that today,
> Upon man's tender feeling grates,
> So they look wise, and simply say,
> He re-hy-poth-e-cates.

92

New labels for old evils. But changing the name of them doesn't remove them nor lessen their consequences in life. Someone said that when the prodigal son fretted at home, wanting to be away, he called what he was doing "independence." That was such a nice name. Out in the far country with bright eyes looking into his, he called it "pleasure." When he lost his money, he called it "bad luck." When he got down to feeding the pigs, he called himself a fool. But when he thought straight about it, he said, "Father, I have sinned." That is authentic.

Let us look again at what the Gospel calls "forgiveness." "I believe in the forgiveness of sin." People have been saying that in the stately creed, for sixteen hundred years. What do we mean by it? Jesus said, "When you pray, Say . . . forgive us our trespasses." What do we mean by the forgiveness of sin?

First of all, it is a pardon. We must begin with that—forgiveness is a pardon, a fresh start, another chance, a new beginning. It is the lifting of a burden, the canceling of a debt, God's answer to the cry of a tortured conscience. "Have mercy, O God, according to they loving kindness, according to the multitude of thy tender mercies blot out my transgressions."

Into the study of a minister came a big, handsome six-foot fellow with all his flags flying at half-mast. In the language of the athletic field, he told his story: "I've been benched for a foul play. Is there a chance for me, or must I sit out the rest of life's game on the side lines?" The minister sat there, listening to a sordid story involving the spoilation of other lives. "How old are you? What quarter of the game is it?" "The first," said the boy. "And that means there are still three quarters of the game to play?" "Yes, sir, three quarters." "And you really want to get back into the game?" "Yes, sir, if the coach will let me." "All right, son, let's get down on our

93

knees here and ask Him." And the great miracle came again, there in the stillness, with no altar but a chair, no ritual but a man making a clean breast of his sins; and then the gladness of heart, the banishment of fear, the release of the pent-up soul in the pardon, in the forgiveness of sin. That is practical enough!

If I were a psychiatrist, I should hardly call it wisdom to ignore this most potent of all relief procedures. Blessed is the man, happy is the man, whose transgression is forgiven, whose sin is covered, in whose heart there is no guilt. Dr. A. J. Cronin was a physician in England until his health broke, and then he became an author. He told the story of a young nurse in charge of a little boy brought to the hospital of which he was the head. The boy was desperately ill with diphtheria; his throat was choked with membrane, and he had only a slender chance to live. A tube was inserted to give him breath, but as the nurse sat by the cot she dozed off, went to sleep, and awakened to find that the tube had become blocked. Instead of following instructions, clearing the tube of membrane—a matter of nursing routine—she lost her head and committed the unpardonable sin of bolting in panic. Hysterically she called the doctor out of sleep, but when he got there the child was dead.

He was angry beyond all power of expression that a child should die so needlessly, by such blundering, inexcusable negligence. Of course she was through; her career was finished. That same night he dipped his pen in vitriol, wrote his report to the health board demanding her immediate expulsion and called her in and read it with voice trembling with resentment. She stood there in pitiful silence, a thin, gawky Welsh girl, half fainting with shame and remorse. "Well, have you nothing to say for yourself?" More silence, and then a stammering plea. "Give me . . . give me another chance."

The doctor was taken aback. Certainly he had no thought of that; it was a breach of discipline, and there was nothing to do but punish her. He dismissed her, sealed his report and went to bed. That night he couldn't sleep. A queer echo of a far-off Word came floating in, kept whispering, "Forgive us our trespasses . . ."

Next morning he went to his desk and tore up the report. Then he went on to tell how this slim, nervous girl became the head of a large hospital and one of the most honored nurses in England. Pardon—another chance—a fresh start:—certainly forgiveness means that. The writers of the New Testament leap to their feet and cup their hands to their lips to shout it; fairly bankrupt human speech trying to express it. Good news: there is forgiveness with God! There is a land of beginning again.

> There is a fountain filled with blood,
>   Drawn from Immanuel's veins;
> And sinners, plunged beneath that flood,
>   Lose all their guilty stains.

Forgiveness—it is the word that rings like music all through the New Testament. It was the impulse in which the Church was born. It was what the early Christians preached about as they went into the fear-haunted, fatalistic, pessimistic Greek world. "Fatalism is a lie," they said, "God gives us another chance." Of course the Greeks laughed at it. To them it was foolishness. Celsus, the Greek philosopher, heaped scorn on their shabby movement. "Every other teacher," he said, "summons to him the best people, the clever and the good, but this crazy Jesus calls to him the beaten and the broken, the ragtag and the bobtail, the failures and the scum." But far from being shamed by that, the Church gloried in it. "Yes, it's true," they said, "Christ does take the broken and

95

defeated, but He doesn't leave them broken and defeated. Out of the failures you would throw away He makes new men; He gives them another chance." Our word "Gospel" means "good news," and this is good news: "Now we have redemption through his blood, even the forgiveness of sin."

But now we must go deeper. Forgiveness that stops with pardon, ignoring the profound, ethical demand involved in pardon, is more immoral than sin. To give a man a new chance without a new heart, to forgive evil without destroying it, to let men off without lifting them up is to demoralize their souls; it encourages them to sin with impunity, and thus make even the grace of God an accomplice of continued evil./Protestants sometimes accuse Roman Catholicism of this. "What's the good of it?" they say. "A man sins, goes to confession, gets absolution, then goes out to sin again because forgiveness has come too cheaply." Of course the Catholics resent the accusation, and I believe rightly so, because it is neither fair nor true to say that the Roman Catholic Church encourages evil. It serves, however, to illustrate a sub-Christian view of forgiveness all too common in Christian history, Protestant and Catholic alike—the disposition to think of forgiveness in terms of safety, protection—to let men off from the consequence of sin without saving them from the sin. It is like the man who was asked by the judge if he had anything to say before sentence was pronounced; the man said it was always his policy to let by-gones be by-gones, and so far as he was concerned, he was willing to drop the whole matter right there. You had better not let men off unless you lift them up!

Two major theories of forgiveness have come down the stream of Christian history, symbolized by two worthy professions—the law and medicine. The lawyer thinks in legal terms and speaks in legal language; God to him is the great

96

Judge and man is a prisoner before the bar of Divine justice, having broken God's law. Christ stands as "attorney for the defense," pleading the sinner's case, canceling his debt, getting the sinner off from the penalty of his transgression. In the language of the court room, he interprets the forgiveness of God. This legal concept has dominated the thinking of theology, or at least the theology of the Western Church, of which we are the offspring. When the Apostle Paul, who was the link between the Hebrew and the Gentile world, entered the cities of the Roman Empire, he translated Christianity from Hebrew into Roman patterns of thought; his language is legal language, his illustrations are legal illustrations, because the Roman mind was a legal mind and thought about everything in terms of law and government. The argument of the Epistle to the Romans is one of justifications by faith—of how God can be just and the justifier of the unjust; it is all legal phraseology.

Then, as the centuries passed and the Roman Church took up the doctrine of forgiveness, it devised an elaborate sacramental system, built around the idea of rewards, penalties, penance, purgatory, confession and pardon, until the great reality was almost lost in the ecclesiastical machinery designed to promote it.

Despite the Reformation, we have largely inherited that legal notion of forgiveness. It is still in our minds to think of it mainly as a means of escape from the consequence of transgression. I am not proposing that we scrap the vocabulary of the law court. What we need most to do, Catholic and Protestant alike, is to get back behind the vocabulary and the machinery to the reality they were originally meant to express. What we need Christ for is not to save us from the punishment of sin but to save us from the sin. That is why, in my judgment, the doctor's mind comes nearer the reality of the New Testament. The doctor thinks not in terms of law but in terms of life. Sin to him is like a disease, destroying life. Forgiveness is the cure of sin, the infusion of a new life to drive the evil out and to restore health and wholeness. Read through the Gospels and, with the exception of a parable or two, you will wonder how anyone could ever have thought of forgiveness as a legal transaction. Jesus went about curing people. He paid no attention to the sacrificial system of the Temple. He got Himself nicknamed "the great Physician."

And where healing of the body ends and the soul begins, who can say? To some people sick in body, He said, "Thy sins are forgiven thee," anticipating by two thousand years that modern psychotherapy which knows well that much of our body sickness is rooted in deeper ailments of the soul. What Jesus was attempting in every case was cure; He seemed to pay no attention to the legal notion. Indeed, he often had to clash with legal minds to work His cure. They brought before Him a woman, taken in sin. "The law says she deserves stoning. What say you?" He didn't answer. Stooping down, He wrote on the ground. When He looked up they were gone; no one was there but the woman. "Where are those thine accusers? Hath no man condemned thee?" "No man, Lord." "Neither do I condemn thee: go and sin no more." You see, they were out to save the law, and He was out to save a life. He came not to condemn, He said, but to save.

But suppose we go deeper still. There is a profound social demand in forgiveness. Forgiveness is *pardon*, and it is personal cure; it is also a process of life and the Christian weapon of social redemption. There is a story of King Albert of Belgium when, in the First World War, as the Germans ravished their little country, the Belgians were bitter and bowed down with sorrow. A small group of children, with their teacher, gathered at a roadside shrine outside the village, kneeling to pray to the Virgin. They were saying the Lord's Prayer; they came to the words, "Forgive us our trespasses as we . . . ," and stopped, choked, and couldn't go on. They were thinking of their country. "But we must say it," the Sister told them, and she went on, "Forgive us our trespasses as we . . .;" she stopped again; another voice took up the words, "As we forgive those who trespass against us." It was their King; he stood behind their kneeling figures with bowed head and burdened heart. I don't see how we can miss this social note of forgiveness. There are sixty-two words for forgiveness in the New Testament, and twenty-two times it means forgive-ness for others. Without that, there is no forgiveness for our-selves.

The one character Jesus pictured as the most impossible to respect is in His parable of the unmerciful slave. You must allow for a bit of humor in this story, and for a twinkle in His eye, as Jesus deliberately exaggerated the details, for no slave in Palestine could owe ten thousand talents, (ten million dollars, someone estimates it) which was more than ten times the total taxes of the country! The slave owed a debt he couldn't pay, not in his whole lifetime and, begging on his knees for mercy, he was forgiven the debt. Then, with all that mercy shown him, he goes straight from his knees to wring the neck of the poor devil who owed him twenty dollars!

Jesus told the story to show that people are not forgiven who are not forgiving; that they have no kinship with the Father unless they possess the Father's spirit; that all of God's forgiveness is wasted on us unless we are moved by His mercy to be merciful. There was nothing legal in His thought about it; if you don't forgive, God won't. He was thinking of the corrosion in the human soul that harbors hate and resentment toward another, and how impossible it is for God's grace to live in a soul that is graceless.

99

Peter had wanted to keep it legal and statistical: "Lord, how often, how often shall my brother sin against me and I forgive him? Seven times?" He knew he had better put it more than three times, which was the customary allowance of the law. He knew he had to be generous with Jesus. "Seven times?" And Jesus said, "Peter, there is no limit to forgiveness. Not seven times, but four hundred and ninety times seventy times seven." In other words, forgiveness is not an act. It is an attitude; it is not a spurt but a spirit. You can't forgive four hundred and ninety times without getting the habit.

Here, then, is the Christian weapon against social evil. We are to go out into the world, we who have been forgiven a debt we could never pay; we are to go armed with the spirit of forgiveness, heal the hurts, right the wrongs and change society with forgiveness. Of course, it isn't practical. Any realist knows that. Life is a matter of—getting even, saving face, being ready to lick all comers—an eye for an eye, a tooth for a tooth. You mean we are to do good to those who hurt us, and after all the vile things our enemies do to us, forgive them? You're crazy. Maybe in some other world, but this is no world to get soft in.

Well, we have been following the practical way for a long time now, and at least we ought to be humble about it and be clear about what this means. The heart of the question is how to get rid of our enemies, or how to get rid of the bitterness that makes enemies. Get that straight and at least you will avoid some of the sentimental caricatures of forgiveness and false application of its spirit. Soft-heartedness is not forgiveness. Soft-heartedness does not get rid of enemies. It feeds them, fattens them, appeases them, and it makes the good in you an accomplice of the wrong in them.

Nor does what is commonly called "non-resistance to evil" get rid of your enemies. How could any one, knowing Jesus, equate the forgiveness He taught with negative non-resistance? No one has ever resisted evil as courageously as He. Principal Jacks said, "One of my teachers in college tried to make a better Christian of me by persuading me to adopt the principle of non-resistance to evil. I was moved to tell him that if he ever detected me in doing evil and failed to resist me to the utmost of his power, using force if necessary, that he was no friend of mine but an enemy of God and a man whom I would denounce at first opportunity." God resists evil. The Cross on the hill outside Jerusalem is the unfathomable measure of His resistance.

The question is—How? How to resist it, cure it, destroy it? One old fellow, interviewed on the radio, said, "I'll be ninety years old tomorrow, and I haven't an enemy in the world." The announcer said, "That's a happy thought." "Yep," the old fellow went on, "I've outlived them all." It's a good trick if you can do it. Narvaez, the Spanish patriot, lay dying, and his Father Confessor asked him if he had forgiven all his enemies. "Father," he smiled, "I have no enemies. I have shot them all." That's an idea too! The Christian technique of forgiveness is to get rid of enemies by getting rid of enmity. In all His teachings about loving your enemies, turning the other cheek and doing good to those who hurt you, Jesus is talking about a wholesome, common sense way of getting along with people, of curing evil at its source and getting rid of the bitterness that sets men against men and nation against nation. The easiest way to do anything is to do it the easiest way, which seems ridiculously obvious but almost impossible for human nature to learn. We have never been big enough to try the obvious so we laugh at it, call it "idealism" and talk it down. But it makes pretty good sense when it gets out of a book into someone's life. Lincoln did it, and because he did it, he holds our hearts in a hush. At the height of the

Civil War, when feeling was bitterest, at a White House reception he dropped a kindly remark about the South, and a woman there flared up, shocked that he could speak kindly of his enemies when he should want to destroy them. Lincoln looked at her and said slowly, "Madam, do I not destroy my enemies when I make them my friends?"

Now, we are not skilled in this technique at all. We have had so little experience in it, even in personal relationships that, collectively confronted with this enormous mass of enmity, bitterness, impenitent brutality, we are profoundly afraid to even risk it. But now we have come to the place where it is a case of "forgive—or else!" These multiplying hatreds can destroy us. This chain reaction of evil—hate breeding hate, wars making more wars, violence begetting violence, eye for eye, tooth for tooth—must be broken. We know, deep in our hearts, that it is no good. We shout loudly about being strong because we fear our weakness, and we build dreadnaughts because our souls are filled with dread.

Bishop Hazen Werner told me recently of a man whose son was among the first to be sent to the Pacific. "Getting on the train at the end of his last leave, there were so many things I should have said and didn't. Now he's going away and I may not see him again. If he's killed, I hope every Jap will die. What am I saying? I can't even think that and be Christian. When he left, I got into my car and drove off into the country, and it kept coming back—'If he dies, I hope every Jap will die.' Forgive me, Lord, for the thought. I fought it. I mastered it. And then a year later, there was the reality. We lost him, but I was ready. I had faced it. We're taking his insurance money and we're putting it into missions for Japan; for what Japan needs, and what we all need, is not more punishment but redemption."

Darkness cannot drive out darkness; only light can do that. More ignorance cannot drive out ignorance; only knowledge can do that. More evil cannot drive out evil; only goodness can do that. Better start with this somewhere tomorrow: "Father, forgive us ours . . . as we forgive theirs."

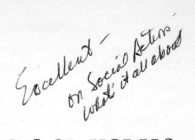

*Excellent —
on Social Action
what it all about*

# SALVATION—MAGICAL OR MORAL?

*and the younger . . . said . . . Father, give me . . . make me . . .*
LUKE 15:12, 19.

IN THE PARABLE of the prodigal there are two petitions which graphically epitomize the two major conceptions of religion. When the prodigal son left home, he said to his father, "Give me . . ." When he came back, humbled, he said, "Make me . . ." So there are those who come to the divine Father, saying, "Give me . . ." Others come with deeper insights, saying, "Make me . . ." And between them is a difference wide as the earth.

Look again at that great word "salvation"—a grand word. It is too bad that it sounds churchy, and that it has the smell of the cathedral on it, for it is not a cathedral word. It did not start in a church or in theology. It started in life and in human need. It has a long and romantic history, around which cluster the human hopes of all generations. When it first came into human speech it was not confined to that one department of life which we call "the spiritual," or to that one section of that department which we call "the soul." It meant deliverance from evil, from all that is wrong in human life and that must be set right. In a sense, the whole history of man is the story of his long search for salvation. Everyone, in some

104

way, is looking for salvation—soldiers, statesmen, poets and prophets, Socialists and Communists, kings and common men. The only difference is in the way in which we seek it, and in how we expect it to come.

There are two kinds of people in the world. (I am almost afraid to say that now, for I read somewhere that there are two kinds of people in the world—those who divide the population into two kinds of people and those who don't.  Just now I am one of those who do.) If you trace the long history of man's search for salvation you will find these two elements and these two kinds of people: those who think of it mainly as a magical process that does something for us, and those who think of it as a power that does something in us. And the great burden of God the Father is not to persuade us to *want* salvation, for everyone wants it, but to cleanse our desire, to purge it of its superstition, to lift us up from the prayer, "God, give me something," to the nobler prayer, "God, make me something." That difference makes a difference, and you can trace it all through human history.

Trace it first in the Messianic hope of Israel and in the *G.* answer of Christ to that hope. He came to a people whose longing for salvation was intense. He found them looking with earnest expectation for a Deliverer, mostly a Deliverer who would give them something, do something for them, change their intolerable conditions. They wanted a military Messiah who would lead in the revolution against Rome and give them back their lost kingdom; they had been taught by their prophets to expect Him. All through their sacred books, like a scarlet thread, there was woven the promise of Someone to come who would sit on the throne of David and bring men salvation. Remember how they sang, waving their palm branches: "Blessed is he that cometh in the name of the Lord."

105

But that hope which in the minds of the prophets had meant an inner, spiritual redemption had been twisted by bitter conditions into a political, materialistic hope. Ground under the heel of Rome, they had come to think of deliverance not from the evil in themselves but from the evil in their enemies; they wanted to be saved from that. They were squirming under the insolence of the Roman conqueror. There were attempted revolutions, here and there. There was a party of Zealots who carried on guerrilla war. When Jesus was born in Bethlehem there were shepherds out in the hills who were sworn under a great oath to start marching when the signal came, and in many a home in Jerusalem were hidden swords and spears and armor ready for that day when the Messiah would come with salvation for the people in His hands.

That was the tense atmosphere in which Jesus began His work. As a carpenter in Nazareth, He had seen it—the hunger, the humiliation, the hurt of it. His heart burned hot within Him, for He was a patriot too, and often He must have felt like Lincoln at New Orleans: "If ever I get a chance to hit this thing, I will hit it hard." He had listened to the flaming speeches of the Zealots. He had seen His people scattered by the soldiers, made to carry their packs for a mile. Often He had seen a cross on a hill where some poor wretch who had talked too much had been liquidated.

He had come to change all that, to be the Saviour, to be the answer of the prophets' hopes and to bring salvation to His people. How? These were the thoughts that burned in His brain as He went down to the Jordan to be baptized. You will never understand the story of the Temptation apart from this. Sitting there alone in the desert with all these things in His mind, He thought it out; He had to choose between the material salvation that the people wanted and

106

the deeper salvation that they needed; He had to make up
His mind whether He would be a Saviour doing something
for them or be a Saviour doing something in them. That was
a real struggle in His soul.

Bread was His first thought. "Start there," the tempter
said. "Command these stones to be made bread." Use your
mighty power to solve the problem of poverty. They will
follow anybody who will provide bread. They always have.
That is how every politician gets his votes; that is how every
dictator rises to power. In fact, the call of bread is so strong
that in our time whole ideologies have been built around the
idea that bread is the most important thing in life. That is
what life is: a battle for bread. And the deliverer who can
solve the bread problem is the only Saviour there is, or
ever needs to be. "Start there," the tempter said; "give them
something. Give them bread. You can control their lives if
you give them bread."

Well, Jesus was concerned about poverty and bread; yet,
sensitive as He was to the material needs of men, He saw
with a profound and realistic insight the great truth which
the whole world now is proving in bitter anguish, namely,
that the bread problem is everlastingly rooted in the spiritual
and that it can be solved only by getting certain ideas and
evils out of people's hearts. "Man shall not live by bread
alone," He said, "but by every word that comes from the
mouth of God." If we would learn the other words—love,
brotherhood, justice—the bread problem could be solved.
No man on this good earth would go hungry if we would
understand these other words from the mouth of God.

So, seeing that what He does for them must be something
done within them, Jesus rejected the materialistic philosophy
that has brought the modern world to suicidal strife.

He rejected the second, too—the appeal to magic. "Give

107

them a sign," the tempter said, "perform a miracle, jump
from a pinnacle. They will follow anybody who will do tricks
for them, or will get things done for them by miracle so that
they won't have to do it themselves." Jesus wouldn't listen
to it. He knew that magic doesn't make people good, that
doing things for people doesn't change their hearts, doesn't
get the evil out. It often puts evil in. It encourages people to
look to God, or to the government to do for them what He
must do within them if they are to be His sons. You can
lump together all the astrologers and numerologists and
spiritualists with all their vulgar panaceas, and test them here
beside this Christ who refused to take that way, even to bring
in the Kingdom of God.

He would not take the sword either. That was the third
temptation—force, compulsion, using the devil's means to
win God's ends. He would not regiment their minds. He
would not force them to obedience. That doesn't make people
good nor help them to change their hearts; He thrust all
that aside as useless to His purpose, and He came out of the
wilderness with His mind made up and clear. He had come
to bring salvation. What He does for people must be something done within them; He cannot give them anything
unless, in the process, He makes them something.

Now let us go on a bit and see this working out in the
history of the Church, which is the extension of Christ's life
in the world. The history of the Christian Church reads like
tragedy in spots, partly because so much of it has been written
by those who had "the gimmies"—by men who conceived of
salvation more in terms of something God does for us than
what He must do within us. All through the history of the
Church we can trace these two elements—the true and the
false, the moral and the magical—"give me" and "make me."

All religions begin in the conviction that something is

wrong in human hearts, and that there is an urgent necessity to set it right. "Thou shalt call his name Jesus, for he shall save his people from their sins." The whole New Testament was brought into being to make that clear. Something new and very wonderful had been done in the world, something that centered in a cross. God had broken into human life to do something for man that man could not do for himself. That was the Gospel, and the first Christians went everywhere with it—unashamed of it because it was "the power of God unto salvation." That is, it saved people, changed them, made them something, cured the evil in their hearts and made them different. It came across the Roman world like a great light shining in the dark. But the old error crept in again and dimmed that perfect Light that came out of Galilee, and in large areas of the earth dims it still.

There is no doubt that in Christianity's conquest of Rome under Constantine our faith suffered a serious twist from which it has not yet recovered. That old superstition which Jesus had so firmly repudiated came back again and into the Church, that trust in magic which is so much a part of man's pagan soul, that disposition to look to some miraculous, ecclesiastical device to change his relationship to God without changing him.

In the Middle Ages the Church built up a vast salvation system—monks, monasteries, creeds and cathedrals, and a sacramental theology for the dispensing of salvation. There is a very old story about a church that needed new hymn-books; a patent medicine company very generously offered to print the new hymnbooks in return for the privilege of putting their advertising in them. But instead of placing the advertisements in the back page or even on the front page, they mixed it up through the hymns. So that on Christmas

morning when the books were presented, the pastor stood up
and read the first verse of the first hymn:

> Hark! the herald angels sing,
> Beecham's pills are just the thing;
> Peace on earth and mercy mild,
> Two for man and one for child.

That is a pretty silly story, but something like that has
really happened to the good news of God as it has come
down through the years. The clear truth of it has become
badly mixed up with the thing it started out to conquer. It is
badly mixed yet, in spots, until, as you look at the historical
expression of Christianity across the years and across the
lands, salvation for multitudes of people called Christians has
come to be little more than a craving for protection, a device
to insure safety from hell and purgatory and the punishment
of sin without saving them from the sin.

What a strange mixture the Church has been, and is! Go
through Mexico and Cuba and South America; see the shrines
there, see the people looking to some magical device for
protection and salvation. A few words pronounced over
communion bread and wine will miraculously transform them
into the actual flesh and blood of Christ, in the taking of
which the "merits" of Christ are legally and officially transferred to the participants to free them from the wrath to
come. A medal, blessed in the name of Christ, becomes a
charm of protection on the highway or the battlefield. Magic!
Children are brought to the church for baptism almost as
automatically as they are brought to the hospital for vaccina-
tion; a few drops of water sprinkled on a child's head officially
transforms him from a candidate for hell to safety in the ark
of God. Salvation by ecclesiastical magic! Good news, and
Beecham's pills!

Nor can we Protestants be smug about that, for the Reformation didn't wholly purify the song. We have inherited, and still hold in our minds, certain mechanical theories of the atoning work of Christ that give altogether too much encouragement to those who want the benefits of the Cross without the battle, who want safety without spirituality, who look to God to change their legal relationship without changing them. Henry Drummond called it "salvation by formula," in which a man, wanting to be saved and go to heaven, is instructed to believe in a set of doctrines, to accept a certain point of view; if he can give mental assent to this, then he has something he is told is salvation. We all have listened to some evangelist speaking on the text, "What Must I Do To Be Saved?" And before he got far, we knew that what he really was asking was, "What Must I Do to Be Safe?" There is a difference there.

Now, all these ideas have truth in them, but they are like that hymnbook—they are a mixture of great truth and magic; they are a confusion of angels' song and Beecham's pills, in which sometimes the pills get the better of it. What we need to do, Catholic and Protestant alike, is to take these great words in which we all believe—repentance, forgiveness, regeneration—and think them out again in terms of reality. We need to get back of all the symbols and the ecclesiastical paraphernalia we have built up to express the thing, and see afresh the thing. We need to free our minds from the mechanical conceptions of the Middle Ages, when God was a static God, and recover the great word He started out to say in Galilee. Open your New Testament. What did Christ come to do?

Certainly, He did not come to bring safety. Nowhere do you hear Him say, "Follow me and you will be safe." He said, "Follow me and you will get a cross." He did not come

111

primarily to save us from the consequence of sin. He came to save His people from their sins—that is, to cure the evil in our hearts, to make us different. He didn't come to get us into heaven. He came to get heaven into us. He doesn't say, "Come with me and I will get you heaven." He said, "Come with me and I will give you eternal life," which is quite a different matter. We are not saying that the desire to go to heaven is unworthy, for it is not. But there is no particular virtue in it, either. Many people want to go to heaven for the same reason they want to go to Florida: the climate is good, and all their kinfolk are there. There are always people who want to feel good without being good, to get something without being something. And Christianity can be made attractive from a selfish point of view. People will follow any preacher or any church that will promise health, happiness or heaven.

We don't need Christ to save us from an abstract, inert substance called "sin"; we need Him to save us from very definite and concrete sin, to cure us of stinginess, fear, selfishness, bad temper, and all that is wrong in me added to what is wrong in you that together makes all the trouble in God's world. And that is what you see on every page of the Gospels —Christ saving people, cleansing them of sin, giving them hope, making them different. He cannot give us anything, not even eternal life, unless in the process He is making us something.

The difference we have been talking about strikes to the very heart of the great social problem of our time and the answers we are bringing to them. We are all looking for salvation now, aren't we? Something is desperately wrong in the world, and there is an urgent necessity to set it right. Millions of good people are working at that, trying to right the wrongs and get salvation for the world. Deep within us now the

Messianic passion burns; people in all lands are crying out like ancient Israel for world deliverance. What kind of deliverance —magical or moral? Something done for us, or something done within us? For what kind of a Saviour are we looking, for someone to change our conditions or someone to change us? You see, the same elements are with us still, and the choice of Jesus in the wilderness is with us still. Christ was rejected by His people, and the world rejects Him still, because His ideas of salvation are deeper and more inward than we care to go. We want God to save us from our troubles, or from our enemies; and He wants to save us from our sins, the sins that make the troubles and the enmities.

That is why our hopes are always betraying us. We still hanker after military messiahs and put our trust in external devices—in law, political machinery and social panaceas. And they are always failing us because they don't go deep enough nor face up realistically to the problem Jesus struggled with in the wilderness—the evil in men's hearts that won't let anything come right.

Now I do not wish to be misunderstood in what I am saying. I am convinced that something must be done for us, and that our leaders had better be about it. I don't want the Church today to play into the hands of those isolationists and reactionaries, for example, who are undermining the United Nations and saying we need no change, no new plans, but only good will. That is not true. We must have plans. We must have political machinery to match the unity that our hope of "one world" has dictated. I believe that is part of God's redemptive purpose too, and we must fight to get it.

The fatal flaw in the plans lies in the fact that they leave out this deeper thing. For the most part, we have plans to change conditions without changing people; most of them are based on the easy optimism that there is no evil anywhere that cannot be legislated away by just passing a law. It is the same old superstition in another form—trust in the magic of law, in our time, almost a synonym for God. Salvation by legislation! You would think we would see through it, after a while. Write a constitution and you have a democracy, enact a prohibition law and you have a sober nation, organize United Nations and, presto! you have a peaceful world! That is superstition too—the same old pagan disposition to trust in external, magical devices to do for us what can only and ultimately be done *within* us, by getting out the evil in our hearts, by driving out false pride, racial arrogance, the desire to dominate and all the other things that make up hell.

We can write the word "peace" in to the documents, but it won't be there if it isn't in our hearts. We can put a temperance amendment in the Constitution, but it won't be there if it isn't in the constitution of the people. We can set up a "New Deal" or a "Fair Deal," but crooked players in the game will ruin any deal. We can scrub the world clean of Communism and pray for bigger and better funerals in the Kremlin, but if all the Communists would obligingly lie down and die tomorrow, the problem would still be there. The world misery that spawned them would still be there, and it will be there until we drive out the evils that breed the tyrants. There is no mechanical device that can save us. There is no magic way to brotherhood. Nothing can be done for us that will redeem us except as it is done deep within our own hearts.

Do you see, then, how we are brought face to face with this Man coming out of the wilderness, His mind made up and clear? Do you see that no one escapes Him or gets away from Him or from the salvation which He offers?

"There is none other name under heaven given among men, whereby we must be saved" (Acts 4:12). If we want a brotherly world, we must be brothers, as He said. If we want to get the evils out of our relationships, we must get the evils out of ourselves. If we want a new spirit in the world, we must be born of His spirit in our hearts. He is the Saviour. He is the great Light shining in our dark. "The Hound of Heaven" has tracked us down. He is calling us by the realities, pushing us by the necessities, luring us by the possibilities, until for the first time in human history the whole world is being judged by Him, and all races and nations, and all classes, are being scourged like the prodigal son barking his shins against defeat and frustration in the far country to go home again and say, "Father, I have sinned. I have lost my way. Make me something. Make me . . ."

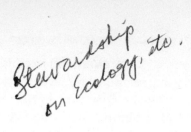

*Stewardship on Ecology, etc.*

# WASTE, WANT, AND WORTHINESS

*...the younger man ... wasted his substance ... and he began to be in want ...*      LUKE 15:13-14.

*Population explosion*

THIS MORNING A six-pound, three-ounce baby was born in a near-by hospital. He is one of ten new arrivals expected in our city today. He is one of about three thousand anticipated, or, as Winchell would say, "infanticipated," in our city this year, one of three and a quarter million expected in America, one of thirty million in the world family. The stork is a busy bird. The world's population is increasing.

About three hundred years ago, for the first time so far as any one knows, a world census was attempted; out of the pooling of incomplete figures it was estimated that, roughly, four hundred million people were then living. Then that number doubled, and doubled again, until today, without accurate figures from some large countries, the estimate is two and a half billions. Before the sun sets tonight, the net gain of the stork over the grim reaper will be approximately ninety thousand.

We are assuming that this newly arrived citizen was born fully equipped with an appetite, a stomach, and a healthy digestive system; and that his first inaugural speech was a loud wail which, being interpreted, means, "Give me food." Where

116

will he get it? He will get it from the earth—by whatever
devious process it is refined. That little body and mind must
be nourished. And everything it takes to feed him, clothe him,
shelter him and warm him will have to come out of the earth.
There is nothing here to feed on except the earth, what it
contains and what it produces, which is the everlasting miracle
of the good earth. The earth is a great pantry which nature
has been storing for millions of years. It is a garden, an
orchard, a granary, a meat shop. In its cellars are fuels, oils,
metals, and everything we need to keep life going. And every
person who comes to live in this world lives off it and takes
something out of it.

Along about 150 years ago, people began to be disturbed
about the twin problems of population and production. A
gloomy Englishman named Malthus wrote a book that frightened men out of their wits. He predicted that the world family
was gradually moving toward global famine and mass starvation. The world was producing people faster that it was producing food and material to support them; he wanted to see
population checked because there was only a certain amount
in nature's pantry. With the population going up and the
food supply going down, the day was coming when there
would not be enough. That frightened people, and set off a
land-grabbing spree of Colonial expansion. Later scientists,
however, disproved the conclusions and premises of Malthus.
They said that he did not have the facts right, and that he
did not have the right facts, that he was judging the whole
world by the two-by-four farming area of England, that he
vastly underestimated the world's resources and man's re-
sourcefulness. Since then, many things have happened to
quiet the fear—the opening up of new continents, the in-
dustrial revolution, mass production, refrigeration of foods,
and many other things which he did not see, nor foresee.

But today that old fear is coming back, and the "ghost of Malthus" walks again; the specter of overpopulation and underproduction is beginning again to haunt us, and questions about the world's waste and the world's want are very much in our minds.

Who looks for the rules of economics in religion? Who would have thought that the world's basic problem of bread would be foreshadowed in a parable? A boy who wasted his substance came to want because he was not worthy of his heritage. Could you get it in a smaller capsule than that? How one would like to walk into the hospitals and homes where these new arrivals have come and, against the background of a great parable, talk straight to them about the world into which they have come and what they must do to live worthily in it!

I suppose the first thing we would say to them is that they must learn to work. The earth that sustains them is rich, but all its riches must be worked for. God created everything, but He manufactures nothing. Our very existence on this planet involves us in a partnership, a divine-human partnership in which we take the raw material which God has bountifully provided and, by the application of intelligence and energy, transform it into bread, buildings, and substance suitable to our use.

We cannot escape that partnership. There is no bread without work, without somebody's work. Somebody has to work to produce the bread. God has ordained as a basic law of life that man shall earn his bread by the sweat of his brow; man must pay his way, must put something in to compensate for what he takes out. And if he tries to live by unearned bread, if he makes no return of brain or brawn for what he takes out, he will sin against his nature and demoralize his soul.

The idea that there is an "upper class," that is, a privileged few at the top who live on the labor of others, is a pagan, immoral idea; it will rot and corrupt any person or social order that holds it. So also is its opposite, the idea that the only workers are those who labor with their hands. Work is the application of human energy, whether it be mental or manual. Brain men without brawn men could not make a loaf of bread. Brawn men without the brain men could not produce enough to keep the human race alive. We must be workers together, and we must be workers together with God.

The first mark of the prodigal mind is the idea that one can be a gentleman and live in the world without work, or on the labor of others. "Give me the goods," the boy said to his father, and went off down the road to spend that for which somebody else had worked. He ceased to be a worker and became a waster. That is what the word "prodigal" means. It is interesting to note the word itself is not in the parable. Jesus did not pin the label on him. We did, and linked it inseparably with his character. He was a prodigal, a waster, not a worker. And it is not surprising that there came a day when he began to be in want, for these two things go together: waste and want, idleness and emptiness are cause and effect. When people take from the table of life without putting anything back they become the kind of people who create want and produce famine in the earth.

Twenty years ago I read a book called *The Economic Waste of Sin*, which pointed out in statistics, (now out of date), that for every man who labors with brain or brawn to improve the world there is another man, a waster, whom he, the worker, must carry on his back. The author went on to show the cost of crime, the liquor bill, the war debts, and so on. Think of the gamblers, the idlers and the nonproductive criminals who prey on society and line their pockets with other people's money! They live on bread for which they have not labored.

> There are a lot of men who creep
> Into the world to eat and sleep,
> And know no reason why they're born
> Save only to consume the corn,
> Devour the cattle, bread and fish,
> And leave behind an empty dish;
> And if their tombstones, when they die,
> Were not to flatter or to lie,
> There's nothing better can be said
> Than that they've eaten up their bread,
> Drunk up their drink, and gone to bed.
>                         (Author Unknown.)

So the first thing we would say to these new arrivals is this: "You are in a partnership. If you don't propose to work here you had better get your robe on and migrate to Mars; you've landed on the wrong planet. This is a work world, and all who live in it must make some return for the space they occupy and for what they take from the table of the earth."

More than that, they must learn to worship, to bow themselves down before the Giver of life and live in appreciation of the gift. Our very existence here involves us in a stewardship as well as a partnership. We do not own the earth, nor any part of it. The earth is indeed the Lord's. The world is literally the Father's house. And every man stands in this planet garden as the first man, Adam, stood in his—to enjoy it, to live on its fruits and to develop his life on it, to care for it and to be the steward and custodian of its resources. Stewardship is no mere dogma of theology. Man's linkage with the land is very real, so real that the earth reflects his moods and his sins. When men come to the good earth like the man with the "green thumb," to co-operate lovingly with its laws, the earth responds in gladness and abundance.

The valleys stand so rich with corn,
They shout and sing.

On the other hand, when men live without a sense of stewardship, without appreciation of the gift of God, when they take the good earth and waste it, they will come to want in it, and the earth will reflect their sins. Cut down the sheltering forests with irresponsible abandon and the earth will answer back in roaring floods. Plow up the prairie grass lands in either ignorance or greediness and the earth will answer back in dust bowls, barrenness, and the creeping death of soil erosion. Stewardship is real enough.

We can never forget the story of the first man. Adam lost his garden and got a wilderness. And in varying degrees man has been doing that ever since, behaving on this planet, not like a steward of its resources but more like a prodigal spendthrift who, having received an inheritance, recklessly proceeds to throw it away and thus destroy the source of his life. That is an age-old story of man's sin against the land and his consequent fight with famine. There is trouble today between Arab and Jew. Through centuries of misuse, lands which in Bible times were rich, capable of supporting thriving cities and teeming populations were drained of their fertility so that men moved out of them, leaving dead cities and vast deserts for their descendants.

Trouble is brewing in Africa; here it is black against white. Alan Paton, in his powerfully moving book, *Cry, the Beloved Country*, dramatized it beautifully. Standing on a grassy hill in South Africa, he looked down into the valley, and in one page of poignant poetry he describes the condition that made congestion in the cities of Africa:

Here on the hills the grass is rich and matted. It holds the rain and mist, and they seep into the ground, feeding the streams in every kloof. Stand unshod upon it, for the ground is holy, being even as it came from the Creator. Keep it, care for it, for it keeps men, cares for men. Destroy it and man is destroyed. But the rich, green hills break down; they fall to the valley below and falling, change their nature. For they grow red and bare, they cannot hold the rain and mist, and the streams are dry in the kloofs. Stand shod upon it, for it is coarse and sharp. It is not kept or cared for, and it no longer keeps men or cares for men. The great red hills stand desolate, and the earth is torn away like flesh. The clouds pour down, the dead streams come to life full of the red blood of the earth. Down in the valleys the women scratch the soil that is left, and the maize hardly reaches the height of a man. They are the valleys of old men and old women. The men are away, the young men and the girls are away. The soil cannot keep them any more.

Reprinted from *Cry, the Beloved Country*, by Alan Paton; used by permission of the publishers, Charles Scribner's Sons.

How closely the great parable fits. A boy who wasted his father's substance came to want because he was not worthy of his heritage, and we waste our substance, and . . . !

Some bitter books are being written now about America, about the waste going on in this rich land, about denuded forests, eroded lands, polluted rivers, dust bowls, tobacco roads, and the uprooted "oakies" wandering about because "the soil won't keep them any more." So we would urge on every new arrival on this planet obedience to what Walter Loudermilk calls "the eleventh commandment"—"Thou shalt inherit the holy earth as a faithful steward, conserving its resources and productivity from generation to generation. If any shall fail in this stewardship of the land, his fruitful field shall become sterile, stony ground and wasting gullies. His descendants shall decrease and live in poverty or perish from off the face of the earth."

And we must say to these new citizens a final and more urgent word. If they are to live worthily here, indeed if they are to live at all, they must learn to love. By the very nature of our existence we are involved in a *fellowship*, linked by a thousand invisible bonds with other people, millions of whom we must learn to love and live with, or collectively destroy the earth in suicidal strife. Would it not be startling to these newly arrived citizens if someone could break the news to them that every baby born here in America starts life owing eighteen hundred dollars—his per capita share of the national debt? Perhaps that partly explains the rising birth rate. Apparently these babies have made up their minds that if this generation is to pay the war debt, there had better be a lot of them. Two hundred and seventy billion dollars! Maybe they should learn to love. The cost of hate comes high.

This has been the most destructive, wasteful half-century in human history. Unable to live in peace with each other, we have squandered our substance with riotous abandon. We went down into the mines, dug out their precious metal and hurled great chunks of it at each other. To preserve our oil we have burned up tons of it—enough to keep our tractors going for a hundred years. To defend our homes we demolished homes, thirteen million homes in Europe, seventeen million homes in Asia; we shattered their cities and scattered their people on the roads, homeless and hungry—thirty million refugees! How long can the good earth stand the cost of hate? How long can the oil last, the copper, and the timber? How far is it to famine in the far country of ill will?

Someone wrote a salute to a nine-inch gun:

> Whether your shell hits the target or not,
> Your cost is five hundred dollars a shot;
> You thing of noise and flame and power,
> We feed you a hundred barrels of flour
> Each time you roar. Your flame is fed
> With twenty thousand loaves of bread;
> Be silent. A million hungry men
> Seek bread to feed their mouths again.
>> From *The Intercollegian*, quoted by Hal Luccock
>> in *Preaching Values.*

Maybe we had better learn to love. The price of hate comes high. We have all seen those charts and figures which try to make our war debt understandable, and show what it would buy in hope and healing. Two hundred and seventy billion! We cannot even imagine it. If you started counting a hundred a minute, kept at it day and night, you would have to live more than five thousand years to even count it. Translated into human terms, it is enough to provide the needy areas of the world with hospitals, schools, libraries, homes, for the next half century. Only that would be foolish spending—it would be "globaloney." Or would it? Put it into plows, seeds, fertilizer, irrigation, reclamation of deserts and wastelands. Then how far would the appeal of Communism go, out in the areas where it gets its converts, if it had to compete with a democracy which had learned to love and conquer the world by serving it, as Jesus suggested?

This is no time for glib language. No one is naïve enough to think that in this sort of world we can lay down our arms. But what troubles us beyond words is the terrific disproportion between what we are willing to do in one direction and what we are failing to do in the direction that matters most. How far is it to famine along our present road, to bankruptcy, to armaments stacked to heaven and at last no security?

The cost of hate is getting higher. A United States senator figured out what it costs to kill an enemy soldier. In Cæsar's wars you could get a good enemy corpse for seventy-five cents. In Napoleon's wars the price went up to three thousand dollars, in the Civil War to five thousand, in World War I to twenty-one thousand, in World War II to fifty thousand dollars. Other statisticians, looking at the whole show, taking the total costs and the total killed in all lands, figured that now it costs the world a million and a half to kill one man. How much to save him? A distinguished official of the National

Broadcasting Company, commenting on that, said, "When we get through with exploiting our resources and exercising our utmost ingenuity in killing men at a million and a half a head, we ought to have brains enough to know how to help men live and be able to show a profit on the operation."

How far is it to famine? We are beginning to feel the pinch of it. Having wasted our substance in unworthy living, we are beginning to feel the want. In diminishing commodities, in the piling up of war debts, the famine has arrived. Maybe that is our hope. When people feel the pinch in their pocketbooks they begin to ponder.

There came a great day for the prodigal son. He began to be in want. He began to think straight. "He came to himself." "What am I doing here?" he asked. "In my father's house there is enough and to spare. Why should I be in want?" There are two kinds of poverty—natural and artificial. And it finally dawned on him that his hunger was wholly artificial, wholly self-made. He was living in a famine which his own folly had produced. It simply did not need to be. "In my father's house there is enough and to spare."

Did you know that a few years ago a geologist of Harvard wrote a book on economics with that as its title: *Enough and To Spare*? The theme of his book was precisely this: that famine in the modern world is almost wholly unnecessary. For the first time in history, man possesses the resources and the scientific know-how to banish famine and to provide all mankind with the necessities of life. This is not a burned-out planet. There are no bottlenecks in providence. To be sure, there are floods and droughts and land erosion which we once accepted as acts of God. But most floods can be controlled, swamp lands can be reclaimed, deserts can be irrigated, top soil can be replaced. Soil men are enthusiastic about what can be done now to replenish the soil. There is no lack of land, twenty-five million square miles of it tillable, of which we are using less than seven million, and much of that not well. A new light has come to man's mind in recent years. God has been good to our age in giving us knowledge of vitamins, nutrition, the chemistry of food, the versatility of atoms. In the suit I am wearing today there is not a stitch of wool or cotton; it is made out of durable substitutes. In Florida, for instance, within the past twenty years, we have had an agricultural revolution. With the introduction of new grasses, new breeds of cattle, the fertilization of pastures, Florida is becoming one of the most promising cattle producing states in the country. Look out, Texas, here we come!

Conservationists believe that, with the new light on agriculture, we have added the equivalent of another continent to the earth. It is literally true that in our Father's house there is enough and to spare, provided we live worthily.

Stanley Jones, speaking on the prodigal, said when the prodigal decided to go home and co-operate with his father, the father threw open everything he had to him—the fatted calf, the best robe, new shoes, his house; in fact, everything the father possessed was the prodigal's when he decided to be a worthy son. What would happen in the world if we learned to live and love as sons? "It is your Father's good pleasure," Jesus said, "to give you the kingdom." What, then, are we waiting for? Technically, the bread problem is already solved. We have the skill if we had the will. What is needed is a new spirit, a new birth, a new life in Christ through which we learn to love.

Our missionaries have been showing the way. They have shown us how to conquer the world by loving it. They haven't had much to work with. But out of the little we have given them they have performed miracles. An agricultural college in Cuba will pay for itself a hundred times over by sending out

Christian-trained young Cubans into the poor areas to tackle the problem of bread. It was a missionary who planted the first apple seeds in Korea. He is an old man now, living in our city—Dr. William G. Swallen, known and loved as "the Johnny Appleseed of Korea." Apples are now a major crop in Korea. For thirty years Dr. Sam Higginbottom, has demonstrated on his farm in India that poverty of the people is not due to impoverished land. With the use of fertilizer, better breeding of cattle, improved methods of agriculture, the land can be made to feed the hungry hordes and have enough left for the sacred cows.

It is not a matter of giving people our resources. It is more a matter of assisting them to develop to the utmost their own. That requires love. When do we start?

*Tops — conversion*

# THE MIRACLE IN THE HEART

*When he came to himself, he said . . . I will arise and go to my father . . .* LUKE 15:17-18.

IT IS NOT easy to come back. Ask any beaten athlete, from blind Samson to Joe Louis; talk with an ex-convict as he looks for decent work with the hands of all society against him; or follow Arnold Toynbee's *Study of History* tracing the descent of civilizations. It is an axiom in the sports world that " they never come back." Long ago the Greek critic Celsus said, "Everybody knows from long experience with actual life that once a man has gone a certain length in sin and folly, there is no smallest prospect of reclaiming him, because inevitably the man is carried down hill faster and faster by his own impetus." But Jesus told a simple story and taught the world to hope; in it was the essence of the Gospel, the good news of which the New Testament is full. Dr. George Buttrick says, "When our clever sciences are forgotten, when all other stories pall, when the earth waxes old like a garment, this story will still be young; it will still have power to untangle our raveled life; it will still win us to our heart's true home."

We are to examine again that miracle in the heart we call "conversion." There is no miracle more wonderful than this; there is no experiment in chemistry more conclusively demon-

128

strated than this; there is no possibility more full of hope for us and for the world than this: that through the love and mercy and power of God the Father we can come back, be born from above and begin again.

I am convinced that many people miss the essential meaning of conversion when it is presented in the pattern of this parable. They miss it chiefly for two reasons. First, they fasten their attention on the coarseness of the prodigal's sins. He wasted his substance, he came to want, he went to the bottom. They have not sinned like that, and with that looming largest in their minds they feel quite remote from him, as though they were made of better clay. Said the Duchess of Buckingham to Lady Huntington, when invited to hear George Whitefield preach, "It is monstrous to be told that you have a heart as sinful as the common wretches that crawl upon the earth."

Then, again, nice people fasten their attention on the manner of his home-turning, coming back in tears and deep repentance, and, inferring that this is set forth as the New Testament pattern of conversion, they shy away from it as irrelevant for themselves. And it does seem, at first glance, that the prodigal's conversion sketches a different portrait from that found in other teachings in the Gospel.

When Jesus spoke elsewhere about conversion there was a touch of beauty in His words. Once He placed a child in their midst and said, "Except ye be converted and become as little children, ye shall not enter the kingdom of heaven." In that, there is a note of naturalness, growth, development, and the clear implication that He thought of conversion as the normal experience of the unfolding life. Just as the seed grows into the plant, as the bud blossoms into the rose, as child life normally matures physically, mentally, and socially, so, if spiritual life be normal, there should be growing surrender to the will of God and gradual unfolding of the Kingdom of

God within. And to be sure, in normal experience conversion should take that gentler form.

When Horace Bushnell, in a former generation, said we ought to expect our children to grow up as Christians and not know anything else, he did not mean that children do not need conversion. He was saying that conversion should not be postponed in life experience until the best years are past, and then have to become a process of rescue, but that it should be as normal a part of the maturing life as the physical development and mental awakening of adolescence. If there is love and worship and reverence and attractive goodness in the home, the child heart opens up normally to the will of God; the new birth for him is as normal as the first birth, and from the beginning he is at home in the kingdom of spiritual reality. Happy are they who have had homes like that and an experience like that.

The prodigal's experience, however, seems to teach another concept. Here is emotional upheaval, deep penitence, soul conflict, drastic break with the past. Unfortunately, the great majority of people have not developed normally in the realm of spiritual reality. Not in all homes do we find love and worship, reverence, and wholesome goodness; and even from homes where they are found some unresponsive prodigals have come. When the normal way has been missed, what then? When the wrong path has been taken, when the spiritual has been neglected or rejected, when the mind has been twisted by a wayward will, when the normal way of coming into the Kingdom is no longer open, what then? Then to come into the spiritual universe does involve a definite, drastic break with the unspiritual past, its sins, its habits, its thought patterns, its ungodlike tendencies. We are strong for the first and normal way. We like the essay the schoolboy wrote on "pins." "Pins," he said, "save thousands of lives

130

each year." When his teacher asked, "How come?" he said, "By not swallowing them." We will vote every time for preventive measures, for the fence at the top of the precipice rather than for the ambulance at the bottom. For, as someone has said, if we would pay more attention to the high chair we might never have to deal with the electric chair.

But the plain fact is that there are many, many people, including a vast number in our churches, who have not developed normally in spiritual things and who do not belong in the first group as they suppose, but who really belong in the second group and need a more definite home-turning than they have yet experienced. They may not have sinned like the prodigal, but, like him, they have sinned, wasted the real substance of life in far lands of secular living, ordering and conducting life as though God did not exist.

Happily, most of us have been delivered from the idea that, conversion, to be genuine, must conform to a certain type. The variety is as wide as the temperament of people. Even among the twice-born whom William James classified as "tough souls," as distinguished from the "tender," there is a wide variety of experience.

Let us begin with those for whom the prodigal provides the most obvious portrait. There are some to whom conversion has come as a cleansing from a life stained and twisted by sin. David knew about that. "Have mercy, O God . . . blot out my transgressions . . . create in me a clean heart . . . and renew a right spirit within me."

"I went down one day to the potter's house," said Jeremiah, "and watched the potter mold a piece of clay. Something in the clay resisted the potter's will and spoiled his dream for it. I saw the clay crumble in his hands and fall in broken pieces on the floor. But he did not throw it away as I supposed he would. Instead, he stooped down, picked up the broken pieces and made it over. The vessel was marred in the hands of the potter, so he made it again." How those old prophets seemed to know the heart of God! How many thousands of people have come to God and had their rebellious clay made over. Every time I go to Chicago, I try to go to the Pacific Garden Mission—not to take part but just to sit among the men and listen. I go because I forget how low human life can sink; I live on a nice street, and I mingle with nice people, and I forget the smells of the far country. I go because I forget how wide is the love of God and how far down its power reaches to redeem.

Thirty years ago I was assigned to lead the singing at this mission one night a week. Vividly etched in my memory is the face of a man who, every Tuesday night, called to broken men to be reconciled to God. He had come up from among them. He used to say that when he was converted he lost sixty per cent of his vocabulary. But God had given him new words. He talked about the Shepherd going out after the one lost sheep. The parable of the prodigal was not lost on those men; they knew who that boy was. With earnestness in his face and voice, he pleaded with them to look to the clean Christ and turn to His Cross. "He can save to the uttermost," he said, "though your sins be as scarlet, they shall be white as snow; though they be red like crimson, they shall be as clean wool."

We must never allow ourselves to forget the husks and smells of the far country, nor must we forget that some of the choicest souls of Christian history were men who came back from swineland to the Father's house. There was St. Augustine, great Catholic scholar of Africa, his mind twisted by an unholy passion. He plunged into the vices of Carthage until he was forsaken by every good friend. Everyone left him except his mother. She stood by. The prolific growth of weeds in his life was evidence of the richness of the soil, and one day he came back, from the depth cried out for cleanness, and the lights went on again in the Father's house.

There was John Newton, son of privilege and advantage, brought up on the English Bible, so saturated with the language of the Bible he could not even swear except in Bible phrases. Early in his life he ran off to sea. Spurning his advantages, he was a wild, reckless, swashbuckling, slave-stealing, drunken vagabond. There seemed nothing left in John Newton to appeal to.

> In evil long I took delight,
>   Unawed by shame and fear;
> Until a new object struck my sight
>   And stopped my wild career.
>
> Amazing grace, how sweet the sound,
>   That saved a wretch like me;
> I once was lost but now I'm found,
>   Was blind, but now I see.

Stories like these could be multiplied out of church history and out of every minister's experience with men. We should not feel too far away from these men, as though they were made of other clay. Who among us does not need the forgiveness of God? We have not all sinned alike, but all alike have sinned. All we, like sheep, have gone astray and stand in need of the forgiving grace of God.

However, as we have already pointed out, it is a mistake to suppose that conversion, or the need of it, is limited to immoral prodigals who have wasted their substance in coarse and fleshly sins. To perhaps a much larger number, it has come as a great awakening, or as the thrilling discovery of a new world of reality to which they have been all but dead. You remember, it was a cultured, respectable ruler of the people to whom Jesus said, "Except a man be born from above, he cannot see the kingdom of God." Men are shut off from God as much by spiritual dullness and unresponsiveness as by immoral crudeness. "Life," said Maltbie D. Babcock, "is what we are alive to." That is, we are alive only in those areas in which we are responsive, and to which we have been awakened. The Bible, speaking of a certain type of social butterfly, says, "She that liveth in pleasure is dead while she liveth." She may be the life of the party in one area, yet be wholly unresponsive in another.

We are all like that to some extent, alive in some things and dead in others. The boy who flunks in geometry because he can't remember the theorem will remember every incident in the ball game and the batting averages of all the players. The man who can remember every fluctuation of the stock market for two years can't remember the text of last Sunday's sermon. Life is what we are alive to. If we had been born here without eyes, much of the world would be shut out. If we had no ears, the whole realm of sound and music would be a closed book. Jesus talked about people who were spiritually dead; their spiritual faculties were dull, they had eyes and saw not, ears and heard not. To be totally submerged in business or the material world is to be just as far from God as to be totally submerged in immorality. Gilbert Chesterton said of Omar Khayyám: "The trouble with the Persian poet is that he spent his whole life in the cellar and thought it was the only room in the house."

To many people, then, conversion has meant coming out of the cellar, awakening to a world to which previously they have been all but dead. One day they came alive to it. One day they lifted up their eyes and saw. One day they turned a corner, perhaps a corner of bereavement, or trouble, and some new insight broke through to them and for the first time they saw. It is true in every realm; there is no arrival without awakening.

Robert Chambers, the Scotch scientist, said the greatest day in his life was the day when he found an old copy of the Encyclopædia Britannica in his attic; for up to that day he never realized there was any such thing as geology or astronomy. He said it was like the opening of a window in a prison through which, for the first time, he saw the world.

Roland Hayes, young Negro boy, came from the backwoods of Georgia to Chattanooga, Tennessee. He walked all the way in his bare feet. To save his shoes, he carried them. He was ignorant and untaught. But he had a voice, and in a church choir a Negro physician heard him sing; the physician took him home with him and played a phonograph for him. And there, for the first time, this ignorant Negro boy heard the voices of Caruso and Melba. "From that night," he said, "I knew I was destined to do something beyond my comprehension. It was as if something was calling me from far beyond the horizon. It was like a religious conversion. That night I was born again. It was like the opening of a door through which I glimpsed the rough outline of the purpose of which is now my whole life. A great happiness came over me. It was as if a bell rang in my soul." Moments there are like that, when heart and brain are clear, when eyes see and ears hear more in a second's tick than in a year.

Horace Bushnell leaped out of his bed one night, seeing for the first time what he had been taught from childhood. "I see it," he said, "I have found it. I have found the Gospel." A new life began for him in that moment of insight, when he saw as reality for the first time what he had known all his life. So many people have found God in sudden insight and awareness. It could happen to you, here and now. There are vast areas of this Christian faith to which some of us have never come alive. New vistas would open up, new understandings would come with new surrender, and we could grow more in a day than in a lifetime. Who among us does not need that kind of conversion?

Now, lest we miss the need of anyone, let us move into a still more universal area. To most people who have found reality in God, including the tough and the tender, conversion comes as a happy release from the tensions of a divided and disintegrated life. Long ago Plato taught that all the disorders of the outer world are but the reflections of disorders in the souls of men. The insights of modern "soul study" have made us acutely conscious of these soul conflicts, and every new exploration into the dim borderland between mind and body brings fresh confirmation of the urgent need in every life for some sort of home-turning, some unifying experience to get the scattered self together.

We have been made familiar with the terms "the split personality" and "the divided self." For illustration, look again at the parable. "When he came to himself, he said . . ." To whom was the prodigal talking? To himself? Certainly. How can a man talk to himself? Does one part of him take another part of him off in a corner to have it out? Why, yes, we are always doing that. That is what thinking is; the "I" is holding conversation with the "Me." For every man is born twins, quarrelsome twins down deep inside of him, wrangling and fighting it out. There is a lower self and there is a higher self. There is a little self and there is a better self. One self in you is reaching for the stars, the other is clinging to the mud; one wants to obey the selfless laws of the spirit, the other seeks to attract attention. The song says:

> One part of me says, Go,
> The other part says, No.

A college professor said:

> I think there must be two of me,
> A living soul, and a Ph. D.

and E. S. Martin sings an oft-quoted strain:

> Within my earthly temple there's a crowd,
> There's one of us that's humble, one that's proud;
> There's one that's broken-hearted for his sins,
> There's one who unrepentant sits and grins;
> There's one who loves his neighbor as he loves himself,
> There's one who cares for naught but fame and pelf.
> From much corroding care I should be free,
> If once I could determine which is me.
>
> MY NAME IS LEGION

That was the prodigal's problem, and it is yours, and every-one's. Something must be done about that tension. The psy-chologists talk about adjustment, and about progressive in-tegration; that is, they say that the divided self must be brought into some kind of singleness of purpose. Some master pas-sion must take over and assume control and organize the mob of conflicting desires into an army of purpose and action. You have to get your whole self going in one direction unani-mously. That is conversion, by whatever name you choose to call it.

There is no hope in surrendering to the lower self, or in organizing your desires around a low objective. That is what the prodigal son tried to do. He said to his lower self, "You take over. Let's get away from this prison house of home with its old taboos and ethical restraints; let's go to places." And then he discovered what millions like him have discovered, that when you try to unify life on lower levels it just won't stay together. It neglects one side of the self, and then one day that neglected side will have its revenge. He could get away from the father's house, but he could not get away from himself.

Nor is there any hope in evasion, or compromise—in one self today and another tomorrow. That is a perfect formula for neurosis. A member of the Mayo Clinic said that doctors there can treat twenty-five per cent of the patients with the physical instruments of science, but that seventy-five per cent of the patients are more difficult to deal with because they are passing on the sickness of their minds and their souls to their bodies, which requires a different approach. Of course, we are not saying here that all emotional and mental sickness is caused by ethical conflict. That would be unkind and untrue. Many factors enter into it. Still, much sickness is caused by such conflict, and drugs can do no good. Nothing you can swallow will unify your soul, nor will analysis alone effect a cure.

We are grateful for better methods, for new insights, for every ray of light that growing science can bring to the understanding of the sick soul. But one thing should be more obvious than it is, and this is that conscience, while often morbid, often overworked, often attached with tragic consequence to trivial matters, has nevertheless an important and God-given function. And consistently to tell everyone with a burdened conscience that guilty feelings should be removed from the mind is to leave many of them with their problems unresolved. The reason some people feel guilty is because they are guilty, and need the forgiveness of God. You would not have helped the prodigal much by telling him that he was the victim of a divided self and must get rid of his sense of guilt. What he needed was to go home, to come to terms with himself, to get straight with his father.

Let us stop here with William James' definition of conversion. He called it "The process, gradual or sudden, by which

138

a self hitherto divided and consciously wrong and unhappy becomes unified and consciously right and happy, in consequence of its firmer hold on religious realities."

Who among us does not need this kind of conversion? And we get it, not by taking journeys, or by talking pills, but by taking a gift—God's gift of forgiveness and the new life in Christ. As another said, "It doesn't take time. It takes surrender."

"I will arise and go . . . ," and he did!

*Beautiful*

# THE SORROWS OF GOD

*But when he was yet a great way off, his father saw him, . . .
and ran . . .* LUKE 15:20.

ONE CANNOT THINK far into the tangled human situation without asking questions about God. How does God feel, looking out on this spinning earth and this sinning human race? Does this world seem utterly hopeless to Him, after long centuries of striving? How does He feel when He hears in it the thunder of guns as men hunt each other down on land and sea and air, and when He sees this beautiful world He has made defaced by strife and lust and human passion? What is the feeling in God's heart? Anger? Disgust? Pity?

You who have seen the Negro play, "Green Pastures," cannot forget the scene in which was portrayed the struggle in the heart of the Almighty, standing with His hands tightly gripped behind His back, torn between justice and mercy—one moment determined to be through with man, leaving him to his own devices, the next wanting to lift him up in His arms and hold him to His heart. How must God feel?

Of course, that goes back to the deeper question, "What is God like?" G. A. Studdert-Kennedy, an English chaplain in the First World War affectionately known to the troops

*What is God like.* 140

as "Woodbine Willie," said that in his experience of three years in the trenches he had come to believe that this was the basic question of life, the question that mattered most to men. What is God like? He said that when he first went to France, before he had seen a trench or heard a gun fired, he went to visit a wounded officer in a base hospital. The conversation turned almost immediately to religion.

What I want to know, Padre [said the young officer] is—what is God like?
I never thought about it much before the war. I took the world for granted. I was not religious, though I was confirmed and went to Communion sometimes with my wife. But now it is different. I have come to realize that I am a member of the human race, with a duty toward it, and that makes me want to know what God is like. When I am transferred to a new battalion, I want to know what the Colonel is like. He bosses the show, and it makes a lot of difference to me what sort of chap he is. Now I'm in the battalion of humanity. I want to know what the Colonel of this world is like. That is your business, Padre. You ought to know.
                    THE HARDEST PART, by G. A. Studdert-Kennedy.

Studdert-Kennedy went on to say that as he followed the men for three years through the mud and blood, he came to see that this was the big question behind all their questions, though it was not always framed that way. What is God like? And not alone on the battlefield, not alone in war, but always and everywhere, this is the big question behind all questions; sometimes it is asked anxiously, sometimes in bewilderment and bafflement, sometimes in bitterness and derision. What is God like? What is the nature and character of the Almighty?

Well, the great word for God on Jesus' tongue was "Father," and it is in that word and in what it means that we must find the answer. There were other words for God before Jesus came — "Creator" — "Judge" — "King" — "Almighty" — and some, in that day, even dared to think that the Power back of life might be like a father. "Like as a father pitieth . . . ," the psalmist said, "so the Lord pitieth." Six times in the Old Testament there are vague, halting expressions of that. But it is humanity's everlasting debt to Jesus that He took this great word, so rich in human tenderness, so familiar to every person (for everyone has a father) and made it the rallying watchword of the new religion, the concept in which we frame our thoughts about God, and taught the halting tongue of mankind to pray boldly: "Our Father, who art in heaven, . . ."

And He will never let you forget that word. There is no sermon in which it does not appear. There is no prayer of His in which it is missed. The first record of His speaking is this: "Know ye not that I must be about my Father's business?" The last word on the Cross was "Father, into thy hands I commend my spirit." When He wanted to tell us what God is like, when men sin and suffer and hurt themselves, He took this word "Father" and wove it into an incomparable, unforgettable story: "A certain man had two sons . . ."

That means that it is given to every parent, in some measure, to know how God feels, what God is like, and to share a little of the risk God took when He made the free spirit of man. And while it is the most joyous view of God that we know, while it gathers up within itself the richest human affections, it also gathers up the poignant feelings that cluster about a cross.

Our subject is "The Sorrows of God." They are essentially the sorrows of a father. Estrangement first! God the Father sorrows over the estrangement of His sons. Here is a little poem on the loneliness of a father, written by Bishop Ralph S. Cushman, which helps us to get into the feel of it:

142

## Life Is So Strange

Life is so strange!
I lay awake last night.
You ask me why?
And I can't tell—exactly,
Only I have lost my boy!

And you won't understand
Unless you too have lost a pal,
A boy, who walked with you the fields,
And jumped with you the brooks,
Together with you climbed the trees.

You watched him as he grew,
You told him all the secrets of the skies
And of your hopes for him.
And, then, one day, you came to realize
That you'd lost your boy!

Yes, life is strange!
I lay awake last night!
How did I lose him?
That's the rub; I lost him
Just as my old Dad lost me.

There came a girl!
And I need say no more.
But just the same
I lay awake last night;
I know I've lost my boy.

Yes, I have lost my pal,
And now I walk the fields alone;
Alone I walk the woods beside the brook,
And everywhere I see old footprints—
Marks of him—but he has gone!

143

I think that in the great Beyond
That there must be a place
Where Dads find once again their pals.
And yet I can't exactly understand
How such a thing could be.
Life is so strange!

> From *I Have A Stewardship*, Copyright
> 1939 by Ralph S. Cushman. By
> permission of Abingdon Press.

You don't go far into the Bible before you run into this, the loneliness of God; it is the kind of loneliness which all parents know in some measure, when they see their children go away from them, set their affections on something outside the home and find their satisfaction and enjoyment in the companionship of others. Even in the normal development of life which the poem suggests, in the dictates of the calendar, in the call of the college campus, in the girl in the next block, even in these normal unfoldings of life it is hard enough to lose your boy or your girl. Sometimes we indulge in the vain wish that they would stay young forever and never grow up at all:

I had a nest full once,
Oh, happy, happy I;
Right dearly I loved them,
But when they were grown,
They spread out their wings to fly.
> —Jean Ingelow.

All parents know about that. But when there is added to that what was in the prodigal's heart—wilful estrangement— there is no sorrow to be compared with it. To bring a child to life and see him grow coarse and cheap and fling away his birthright like a fool; to dream the best for him and then see him choose the worst, to crave companionship with your children and get indifference, to long for affection from them and get ingratitude—that hurts! A broken-hearted father said that he had planned and saved and worked to make his home an attractive place for his boy, but had failed, for all his son's thoughts and interests were outside the home in a world of which they, the parents, knew nothing at all. And he said the breach was widening between them as though, under the same roof, they lived in two different worlds.

That, too, is the hurt in the heart of God, that His children so often find their interests and lay their plans outside His love and will. It made the prophets downright angry to see the people He had chosen to be His people give the devotion of their hearts to false and foreign gods. "I have nourished and brought up children, and they have rebelled against me. The ox knoweth his owner, and the ass his master's crib: but Israel doth not know, my people doth not consider" (Isaiah 1:2, 3). "I taught Ephraim also to go, taking them by their arms, but they knew not that I had healed them" (Hosea 11:3). That hurts. I believe that is back of a sharp word Jesus once spoke to some very respectable gentlemen. "You," He said, "are of your father, the devil." It was the boast of the Pharisees that they were well-born folk, that they were sons of God because they were descendants of Abraham. But Jesus said bluntly, "You are of your father, the devil." What did He mean by that? Certainly He did not mean that the devil had ever created anybody or cared for anybody. It was rather that in their interests and spirit they were so alien from the spirit of the heavenly Father that they were more the children of evil than the sons of God. Let me illustrate.

In a western town lived a preacher whose son grew up tall and straight, with a mind keen and clean and wholesome. In that same town lived a foul-mouthed, atheistic, and very brilliant doctor. A strong friendship grew up between the two.

The doctor, with his brilliant mind, became a hero to the boy, and gradually there came an estrangement in the preacher's home. Under the father's roof the boy was irritable and unmanageable, contemptuous of his father's faith, resentful of even his mother's kindly concern. And wherever the interest of his father came into conflict with the interest of his friend, the boy consistently chose the latter's way and soon came almost completely under the spell of his atheistic hero, so much so that the people of the church shook their heads sadly and said, "He is getting more like the doctor than like his father. He is more the doctor's son than the son of his own father."

One midnight the preacher, with heavy heart, stole softly into the bedroom of his son, to find the air filled with the fumes of alcohol, and the boy's mother kneeling by his bed, stroking his hair, kissing his forehead, caressing him. Looking up through the veil of tears, she said, "He won't let me love him when he's awake."

That is one of the dominant notes of Scripture, from the first Book, in which you hear God say, "Adam, where art thou?" to the last Book, in which you hear Him say, "Behold, I stand at the door and knock." The loneliness of God, the sorrow in God's heart! That we should seek life's satisfactions, center our affections, look for our enjoyments outside His loving will, and have no fellowship with Him who is our Maker and our Father—that is what hurts Him!

Now we must go a bit deeper, for the sorow in God's heart is not alone from our estrangement but also from our impoverishment, the wide gap between what He has dreamed for us and what we have done with the dream. He has put immense possibilities into all things, including human life, and provided all the resources for immeasurable achievement. And He waits hopefully for us to take His gifts.

Lord Chesterfield was a man of many gifts; he was not a good man but a gifted man, and most of his gifts were devoted to the careful, supervised training of his son, who he expected would be a genius. The boy grew up to be a useless nonentity. With all the advantages and resources of a rich tradition, that is what came of it—nothing.

You keep running into that all through the pages of the Bible; the Book pictures endlessly the disappointment in God's heart that so little should come from His expectations and investments. That is part of the pain that made the Cross. It was amazing to Jesus that men would not avail themselves of the promises and privileges which God so lavishly offered. He seems to be forever saying, "You will not come unto me that you might have life." Right at the height of the Palm Sunday procession, He looked out over Jerusalem and wept. "O Jerusalem, Jerusalem, how often would I . . . and you would not. He put it all down in the parable of the barren fig tree. Israel was the fruitless tree. This nation which was preparing to kill Him as they had killed the prophets before Him, this nation which God had privileged above all nations, which had been cared for and cultivated as a chosen vineyard of the Lord, had brought forth nothing. "You will not come unto me that you might have life." That is the eternal heartbreak of God.

But the deepest lesson of the story, and one which we can hope to understand only as we think of God in terms of "fatherhood," is that God the Father Almighty sorrows and suffers in our defilement. Lift up this great sentence and take a long look at it, for it holds the answer to many a baffling question: "When he was yet a great way off, his father saw him, . . . and ran . . ." Was it an accident that he happened to be on the roof top that evening, looking down the road?

On the wall of the Sunday school which I attended as a boy

was an old-fashioned picture of a young man playing chess with the devil. The young man's soul was the prize of the game, and the devil was winning. It was the boy's move, and judging by the position of his pawns, it could well be his last move. Beads of cold perspiration stood out on his brow as he studied his move and looked across the table into the leering face of the tempter. But what gave meaning to the picture was that dimly shadowed in the background was the face of God and the figure of a cross. Old-fashioned as that picture was, it profoundly symbolized a reality which no human words can express: the haunting certainty that we are not alone in the game, that Someone seeks us, pursues us, follows us, suffers with us and for us in our sinning. God is not far off in His heaven somewhere "contemplating all"—as Tennyson has it in his *Palace of Art*. He is not outside the world looking on in cold, majestic aloofness. He is here on all the roads of life, living in our living, striving in our striving, identified with us in our defilement.

What else does the Cross mean? "God was in Christ reconciling the world unto himself." "He was numbered *with* the transgressors." "He was wounded *for* our transgressions." "He bore our sins *in* his body upon the tree." What do these great words mean?

Controversy has swirled for centuries around the idea of omnipotence. What is power? What is almightiness? What do we mean when we say, "I believe in God the Father Almighty"? It is really pathetic that in two thousand years we have learned so little about the deeper meaning of the Cross which Paul said was the power of God—God's kind of power. From the questions some people ask about God, it is evident that their ideas of almightiness must be overhauled. They think of God in that "king" framework—as an almighty monarch sitting on a throne, with the earth as His footstool trembling beneath His feet, getting what He wants done by miracle or a wave of His hand or a nod of His head. With that image of almightiness in the back of their minds, they pray foolish prayers and ask foolish questions. Why doesn't God stop wars? Why doesn't He break in and smash the schemes of wicked men? Why doesn't He come in power and glory, put an end to human tragedy, get His will done? Yet the years roll on and nothing happens. No Voice speaks from the silence. Maybe He is not almighty. Maybe God is helpless when things go wrong and cannot control what He has made.

H. G. Wells thought so. In his book, *God the Invisible King*, he pictured the unseen Power back of life as a kindly, lovable Soul who desperately wants to make a good world with peace and love in it, but He can't do it. The world has gone too far; it is out of hand, beyond control. And so Wells pictures the Almighty standing in the wings, trying to keep the play going and the scenery from falling in, calling frantically to us human folk to come and help Him. Poor Mr. Wells!

If we wonder at times why evil is not more firmly and effectively controlled, we should stop and think through the implications. What would we have the Almighty do? Kill off the wicked? How? Earthquake? Fire? Lightning? Suppose He should. Whom would He kill? The bad men in the Kremlin? But after them, whom? Where would He stop? Look out now. If God should run His universe on the basis of the almighty monarch, purging and killing off those who sin and defy His will, none of us would live to be full-grown.

Of course, we don't mean that exactly. What we wish is that He would exercise His power more and break in and change wicked hearts. But look out for that, too! Who, then, would be free, and in what would freedom consist? Would there be any freedom at all? No, you have to come to this:

149

God the King Almighty would be a despot, a dictator and not a father at all.

Here is the truth: "When he was yet a great way off, his father saw him . . ." Here is the great heart of the Gospel. God has not made us puppets. He has made us persons, with all the risk of it, free to choose the good and therefore free to choose what is not good. What seems a limitation in God is a limitation He has imposed upon Himself, the kind of limitation all parents, in some measure, must know. He will not thrust Himself upon us. He will not impose His will upon us. That same father who respected the prodigal boy's rights when he went away, who refused to coerce and restrain him, never lost his son out of his heart. He followed the boy in all his shabby defilement; he stood like a haunting shadow behind the boy as he lost out in the game of life; and when he came to himself and turned his feet at last back to the father's house, the father was waiting with forgiveness. "While he was yet a great way off . . ." Oh, the restraint of God, the almightiness of God! He who could crush us, yet stoops to beseech us.

A friend of mine, the late G. W. Rosenbery, told me a story out of his early ministry. He was in a railway coach speeding across the state to attend a conference. Few people rode on trains in those days, and one boy in his late teens, apparently very nervous, attracted the attention of his fellow passengers. The boy was fidgety and restless. He would sit in one seat for a few moments, then move down the car to another.

The minister began to watch him and study him; finally he sat down beside the boy and said, "What's troubling you, son? Worried about something? Maybe I can help you. I am a minister, and if you feel like telling me, I should like nothing better than to help you if I can." "Sure, sure," the boy said, "I don't mind telling you. Are you acquainted in a little town named Springvale?" "Well, not exactly. I know of it. It is the next stop, isn't it?" "Yes," said the boy. "We'll be there in fifteen minutes. That's my home. I used to live there. My father and mother live there still, just a mile on this side of the town. Three years ago I had a quarrel with my father. I said, 'You'll never see me again.' I ran away from home. Three years, and they've been tough years. Sometimes I wrote to my mother. I wrote her last week and told her I would be on this train passing through. I told her I would like to come home just once; asked her if it was all right for me to stop, to hang something white outside the house so that I would know that father had agreed to let me stop. I told her not to do it unless father wanted it. She would do it regardless, you know, but I had to know how Dad feels."

The boy looked out the window, then started up excitedly. "Look, sir, my house is just around the bend, beyond the hill. Will you please look for me, see if there is something white? I can't stand to look. If there isn't anything white—you look, please!" The train lurched a bit as it made the slow curve, and the minister kept his eyes on the round of the hill. Then forgetting his dignity, he fairly shouted, "Look, son, look!" There stood a little farmhouse under the trees, but you could hardly see the house for white. It seems that father and mother had taken every bed sheet, bedspread, tablecloth, pillowcase, and even handkerchiefs, and hung them out on the clothes line and the trees. The boy's face went white, his lips quivered. He couldn't talk. His nervous fingers clutched the cheap suitcase, and he was out of the car before it had wholly stopped at the water tank. The minister said that the last he saw of him, he was running as fast as his legs could carry him, up the hill to the little house where the white sheets fluttered in the wind.

There are many elaborate theories about the meaning of the

Cross, and profound words are needed to express it. But we are grateful, too, for a simple story which vividly tells us that the white sheets are out on the eternal hills of God.

"When he was yet a great way off, the father saw him, . . . and ran." Some of you ought to come Home. You have been a long time away.

*Easter*

# THE DEEP ROOTS OF JOY

*This my son was dead, and is alive again; he was lost, and is found. And they began to be merry.*     LUKE 15:24.

FOR CHRISTIAN PEOPLE the most thrilling day in the world is Easter Day. It is the day of trumpets, music, glory and gladness—"when everything that hath breath shall praise the Lord." Fresh as the springtime, it comes each year with a mystic, inner joy in which all nature joins in a fresh renewal of life. For what we celebrate in Easter is not immortality alone, nor even the resurrection of Christ alone, but a whole philosophy of life that stems out of it, of which the Resurrection is the symbol and the promise.

Easter means to us exactly what it meant to the first Christians, not merely the assurance of survival in another world but the still more exciting possibility of rising out of our dead selves into newness of life in this world. You get a hint of it in the parable. "This my son was dead, and is alive again. . . . And they began to be merry." These twin truths are eternally linked together—the renewal of life and the release of joy.

It is an amazing thing how Christianity ever got the reputation for being gloomy. In an essay on "The Lost Radiance"

153

Dr. L. P. Jacks said, "Christianity is the most encouraging, the most joyous, the least repressive of all the religious of mankind. While it has its sorrows and stern disciplines, the end of it is a resurrection, not a burial—a festival and not a funeral." "They began to be merry . . ." We shall not waste time to point out the error of medieval art and theology which made Christ a mournful man without a smile—a pale Galilean, according to Swinburne, "who has made the world grow gray at His breath." That is heresy. We have not so learned Christ. The fact is, there were times when He had to defend Himself from the accusation of His enemies, who complained that He was much too cheerful to be a holy man.

Dr. Arthur Gossip has described the New Testament as "the happiest thing in literature, with the sound of singing in it everywhere, opening with the choir of angels over Bethlehem and closing with the Hallelujah Chorus of the redeemed."

Nor shall we stop here to appraise the joylessness of much of our modern Christianity except to say that that, too, is, in part, heresy. A gloomy Christian is a contradiction in terms. The young son of Bishop Charles L. Mead sat in the front pew in church while his father preached. He was looking up at the proscenium arch over the pulpit where there was a row of lights; he had named each light for a Book in the Bible— Isaiah, Jeremiah, Lamentations, Ezekiel, and so on. At home after church, the little fellow was distressed, and his father asked, "What's troubling you, son?" He said, "Daddy, Lamentations has gone out." Well, Amen! Let it go. We could do with less lamentation and more laughter in the house of the Lord. While there is much in the world in which no Christian can rejoice, if we fall into depression we have lost our Christian credentials. Christianity is a joyous faith.

It is important, however, to distinguish clearly between the joy of Christianity and what the world calls happiness. The

154

New Testament talks much about joy but very little about happiness. And there is a difference between knowing how to laugh and knowing how to rejoice. We live in a generation in which happiness is pursued with a kind of grim desperation, mainly because men and women, having detached themselves from the source of the real thing, are obliged to devise substitutes and are feverishly trying to produce fruits without roots.

The joy of the New Testament is rooted deeply in spiritual reality. It is rooted, first of all, in *righteousness*, in *rightness*, in *harmony*. Wherever you find rightness, you find a release of joy. The Greeks had a word for it. They called it "euphoria"— that wonderful sense of well-being and exuberance when all is well without and within. It is what Browning described in "Pippa Passes":

> The morning's at seven,
>    The hillside's dew pearled;
> God's in His heaven,
>    All's right with the world.

It is what you feel when the star of "Oklahoma" sings:

> Oh, what a beautiful morning,
>    Oh, what a beautiful day;
> I have a wonderful feeling,
>    Everything's going my way.

It is that mystic harmony the poets feel in the pageantry of nature—"the morning stars sang together"; "the trees clapped their hands"; "the hills shouted with gladness." This is pure poetry, yet it is not without reality. There is a gladness in creation, the sound of harmony and singing of which even we, with our dull ears, have heard a few stray notes. Emily Dickinson said, "If God had been here last summer and had seen some of the things I saw, I am sure He would have thought

His upper heaven superfluous." There are times when we feel at one with all creation in a wonderful sense of well-being, and when all is well without and within.

What puts gloom in God's world is wrongness, sin, and disharmony. "Unhappiness," said Dr. Hocking, "is dividedness of mind." Sorrow is the feeling that comes from disharmony, from something wrong within the heart and without, in its attitudes or relationships, like the sorrow of the disciples that Good Friday night when they fled to the hills terrified and bewildered. What shook them to the depths was the paralyzing fear that there was no rightness in God's world, that their trust in rightness was an illusion. Underlying everything their Master had taught them was His unswerving sureness that this was God's world . . . and it wasn't. He was mistaken. Nothing made sense; there was nothing to believe in, nothing to count on, nothing to do except what the sobbing women had found to do—prepare spices for His burial, sit by the tomb in sorrow.

Every once in a while someone writes it down that the Resurrection story is a myth, that someone made it up, and that there was no empty tomb. But we go laughing in our hearts because we know that is a lie. Something happened in that garden that transformed deep gloom into exuberant gladness and turned a handful of hopeless, defeated men into the nucleus of the Christian Church and the forerunners of a new order on earth. Dr. Luccock tells of a man looking for the first time at the stupendous spectacle of the Grand Canyon, Colorado. After his first gasp of silent awe, he said, "Something must have happened here!" It was a bit obvious. That cut in the earth 217 miles long, from four to eighteen miles wide, and in places more than a mile deep, was not caused by "an Indian dragging a stick along the ground." When Ring Lardner saw it for the first time he thought it was an excellent place to throw old razor blades. Something happened! Mighty effects call for mighty causes. Something happened in Joseph's garden, and the first effect of it was to restore the disciples' shaken confidence in the rulership of God and the rationality of life. The world was not mad, not careless, not capricious, not unpredictable. There was *rightness* in it, and all the power of God was back of that rightness.

The New Testament rests solidly on the conviction that the world is ruled not by fate nor by blind chance, but by one Mind, one Spirit, the righteous will of God of which our "laws of nature" are the expressions. And wherever we relate ourselves to that rightness there is a release of joy—in music, in art, in all the upward strivings of man's heart. When we relate ourselves to the law of love and live by the law of service, we find joy in giving. "It is more blessed to give than to receive." When the right girl comes along, God puts the sound of laughter in the heart. Joy and love are linked together in a wonderful "euphoria." You never have to ask God to come to a wedding. He is there. "Ah, sweet mystery of life, at last I've found you." Something just right!

Even when we relate ourselves to the physical energies, there comes a joy of discovery which is part of the gladness of creation. Some years ago there was a man in my church who had given his life to research and invention. In his earlier years he had searched long and painstakingly for a better way to get dust out of rugs than to hammer it out with a rug beater. And when at last he found it, he shouted, "Eureka," even as Archimedes shouted centuries before, "I have found it." And he passed that name on to his vacuum cleaner. When Sir Isaac Newton discovered the secret of gravitation he was so excited and overjoyed that he could not write down the principle for trembling. He had found the way life works and holds together.

157

Our modern day has been full of exciting discoveries. We have found that when we relate ourselves to a certain *rightness* in God's world, we can harness powerful energies—"all going our way," as Emerson said. So, sensible man now believes the physical world is ruled by chance. An immense confidence has grown up in its trustworthiness, and in the idea that we can perform near miracles when we go along with the way life works.

This is true also in the realm of the spirit. The joy of conversion is like that. When the soul returns to its true home, when we find Christ as the way of life, when we relate ourselves to His will, joy springs up naturally in our hearts. "They began to be merry." That is an authentic word. The lights went on in the father's house because something wrong had been made right and a broken relationship had been restored. The world was different for the prodigal because he was different. Everything was right because he was, and there was music and dancing. Joy is rooted in *rightness*.

It is also rooted in reconciliation and reunion. That is what the New Testament means when it assumes that some of our richest joys are born not of laughter but of pain, of our involvements in the lives of other people. We have all known this gladness when a loved one, long ill, gets well; or someone long absent comes home. Jesus, I think, believed that the music of heaven is made out of the tears of the reconciled. This parable of the prodigal is one of three parables, all of them about lost things. When the shepherd found his sheep, he rejoiced in the restoration. When the woman found her coin, she said, "Rejoice with me." When the son came home, there was music, made in part of tears and in part of laughter. And Jesus felt that the joy of reunion makes the angels sing.

At the close of the last war, when our great civilian army

was being demobilized and the men were coming back, Theodore Maudlin wrote a happy little story:

My wife and I were calling the other day on a young woman whose husband had been three years overseas. We sat on the porch while she was preparing some tea for us in the kitchen. We saw a young man in uniform walk toward the house and stop at the gate. For a long moment he looked up at the house, then came up the steps, paid no attention to us, and walked in the door. He quietly set his duffle bag down and listened to the rattle of cups in the kitchen. Then he whistled softly an old tune, and the noise in the kitchen stopped. Then we heard her moving toward him in the hall. There they stood a few feet apart, their hands touching. No words were spoken, but all that two people could say with their eyes was said. He cleared his throat, then slowly reached down into his duffle bag and brought out a box. With superb calmness, he said, "Darlin', here's the candy I went out to get for you." Her eyes were filled with happiness, framed in a crystal circle of tears. But when she spoke, her calmness matched his. "Thank you, dear, but I think you were a long time getting it." Then they were in each others arms, and we tiptoed out the gate.

I have always been glad that the great words of our faith are family words—Father, Son, Love, Home. Our lives are richly blended in other lives. And out of these human ties come both our laughter and our tears. This foolish boy of the parable left home seeking happiness in independence from human ties, only to discover that the soul cannot make its own music and that real joy is not in renunciation but in reunion.

Here too is the trumpet note of Resurrection—reunion, glad reunion with those loved long since and lost a while, reunion on a higher level. "Then were the disciples glad when they saw the Lord." He had come back to them, to the same Christ. Yet he was not the same. How the questions swarm around that! You and I cannot picture a Resurrection or visualize a Resurrection body. But what is the difference?

159

You and I cannot visualize an electron, either. Invisibility does not mean unreality.

Our ability to picture or to prove what happens at death or beyond it is just where it was two thousand years ago. But so also is the hope and the promise. We do not know where heaven is or what it is like, and we must be faithful to our ignorance. Some of us are inclined to believe that heaven is the whole universe of God. God has one universe and there are certainly many places in it. We cannot believe that this little earth is the only world, or that it is the most important world. Jesus said, "In my Father's house. . . ," taking up the idea of the parable. "In my Father's house are many rooms, or places, or mansions." We are not worried about overcrowding there, and we are not troubled about recognition. To us the survival of life there is not one whit more mysterious than its arrival here. Home means reunion. In the Father's house there is love, laughter, music. The many mansions are lit up, and "in His presence there is fulness of joy."

But the Easter trumpet sounds another note. Joy is linked with and rooted in redemption. "This my son was dead, and is alive again." When you get back of the rapturous language of the New Testament epistles you find that it springs out of a renewed faith in human life and its exciting possibilities. To the folks of the New Testament, the Resurrection was not an isolated incident in a garden that happened once and for all. It was also a symbol of a new aliveness in their own experience. "We have passed from death unto life. We have come alive. We who were dead in wrong ways of living and thinking have been raised to walk in newness of life." Christ had wrought in them a change so real, so deep, so joyful, that it was like a new birth out of the darkness of death into the light of life. Because of what happened in them they came to think of the Resurrec-

tion as a continuing force, which would keep on happening
to people until the whole world should be reborn.

If our poor, tired generation could recapture that faith and
sound that note again it would turn our *misereres* into halle-
lujahs. Most of our current social pessimism grows out of a
certain fatalism about life, chiefly about man. Millions of
modern people have grown fatalistic about human nature.
"See," they say, "how stubborn, recalcitrant human nature
spoils all plans and blocks all progress." The world would be
right if the people in it were. And that, they say, is what you
cannot change—people.

Now, that fatalistic type of thinking is the surest road to
gloom and pessimism. I tell you, it is not Christian. It is not
factually true. The first Christians would never have subscribed
to it. Because they had been changed, they believed all men
could be changed; because Christ had transformed them, they
believed all men could be transformed; because God was in the
world, and men were made to be His sons, because a new creative power had been released in His world, anything could
happen in it and all the doors of possibility were thrown wide
open. It was that buoyancy of spirit, that sublime confidence
in common people, that laid its hand on a tired and decaying
society and made it take heart again. Eleven men with a bit
of good news did change the course of history. Fate doesn't
make history. People do—people, and what they believe.

Let me close with a story. The chaplain of West Point
Academy told of a young, skinny G.I. who walked whistling
into a New York book store. The girl behind the books said,
"My, but somebody's happy!" "Sure," he said, "I've just come
back from Europe. I spent a year in a German prison." She
said, "That should be enough to make any fellow happy."
"Well," he said, "it wasn't that. I've come to get a book. In
the prison we didn't have much to read and one day someone

handed me an old, dog-eared copy of a religious novel that I would never have bothered to read if I had had anything else to read. But this book told how everybody who came under the influence of Jesus had wonderful things happen to them and how it helped them to start living a new life. And, you know, it happened to me, there in the prison. I was set free in my heart before the army set me free. When I came home to my wife—she's really pretty and sweet and all that—but you know, she's lacking something. She's downhearted and scared and sort of bound up in herself. So I've come to get a copy of that book. I want to read it to her. I want to happen to her what happened to me."

Do you think the Resurrection is something far off, in a garden long ago? Well, it is. But the good news is that it is still happening, still happening in the lives of people. It happens when they relate themselves to the *rightness* which is revealed in the Christ who is the Lord of death and life. It could happen to you!

# THAT FELLOW WHO STAYED
# AT HOME

*Now his elder brother was in the field: . . .*

LUKE 15:25.

IT WAS A marvelous story Jesus had told; Dickens called it, "the most touching story in literature"; George Murray said, "It is the most divinely tender and humanly poignant story ever told on earth." Even the Pharisees softened under its spell. Everybody does.

The story takes hold of us. Just read it without comment, and you will find every line of it making for the heart. A boy saying, "Give me . . ." to his father, chafing under home restraint, wanting to get away from it all; life calling, laughter, music, dancing, the lure of the far country—how human it is!

But there is a Law, an eternal, inescapable law. "There arose a famine in that land." An empty stomach becomes a preacher of righteousness. "I'll get up and go home." Trudging the homeward path, between sobs he made up a speech. He had made such a sorry mess of freedom. He was willing now to trade it for bread or a job. "Make me a hired servant." And the father, who is the real hero of the story, with a love the boy never understood, sitting on the roof-top, watching the

163

road, then running to meet him. The speech was smothered in a choking sob.

> For the love of God is broader
> *Than the measure of man's mind;*
> And the heart of the Eternal
> Is most wonderfully kind.

Get some decent clothes for him. The boy is home again. "They began to be merry."

This is a grand place to stop. Even the Pharisees were nodding their heads, and it is a good time to stop when the audience is in agreement. But Jesus didn't stop there. He couldn't. He went on to describe another sinner—the fellow who stayed at home. He had to. Remember why He told the story in the first place? Why He told three stories, in fact—the story of a lost sheep, the story of a lost coin, and the story of a lost son? The breach between Him and the Pharisees had been widening. Their hatred for Him, at first held in check, now was beginning to blaze in the open. They had assailed Him, among other things, for conduct unbecoming a religious man—for companionship with the outcasts. "This man eateth with publicans and sinners." It was unheard of, and it could not be tolerated; they were mumbling in their beards about it. So He spoke this parable unto them, "What man of you, having a hundred sheep, if he lose one doth not leave the ninety and nine to go after that which is lost?" That is, is it not a normal instinct in a shepherd to protect his property? Or when people lose money, is it not a normal human instinct to search for it until it is found? And when it comes to human life in any decent home, what father among you would not feel as this father felt, when his wayward boy came back? In other words, Jesus is saying, in effect, "You Pharisees are finding fault with me for doing what every normal human instinct would lead anyone to do. Is it immoral in me to be concerned about these prodigal people who have made a fleshly mess of things? But you Pharisees, what sort of religion have you made for yourselves? A religion that cares nothing about lost people? You have said what you think of me. Very well. Now let me say what I think of you. Stand up, while I draw your portrait! The elder son was in the field: . . ."

It is surprising how little study we have given this elder brother. We nearly always think of him as an anticlimax. We nearly always stop with the return of the prodigal, with the vague idea in the back of our minds that when we have reached that place we have preached the Gospel, and that if we could persuade all the prodigals to repent and come home our evangelistic obligation would be fulfilled. All of which reveals how inadequate is our conception of the range and depth of the Christian message. We don't give enough thought to the disturbing possibility that Christianity is a much bigger thing than we have made it or imagned it; consequently, we have never seen this elder brother for the downright sinner he really is, and how far short he, and we, have come by the test of the real Christian standard.

We usually think of him as a man who did pretty well, certainly in contrast with his brother. He was at least respectable; he had stayed decently at home. He had some virtues our age admires very much. He was thrifty, industrious, dependable—eligible for membership in the Rotary Club or on the Board of Stewards of his church. That is what a low estimate of Christianity does. It sees a lot of people in the fold who are not in but shut out by sins we have not been morally sensitive enough to call sins. At any rate, we make a great mistake when we set this respectable elder brother up as the bright background against which the prodigal's blackness is painted. We are nearer the truth when we regard him as another kind of sinner to be evangelized.

Let us begin with the most obvious fact about him—that, for all his respectability, he illustrates a kind of ungracious, unattractive goodness that is much too common. True, he stayed at home, did the chores, kept the rules, performed his duty. He sowed no wild oats, wasted no money nor scarred his soul with dissipation—all of which was definitely in his favor. But he was a sourpuss, none the less. Not the kind of man you would want to go fishing with, not a good example of righteousness; touchy, stingy, churlish, thoroughly wrapped up in himself, he did the right things, all of them in a wrong spirit that repels and pushes you away.

Roy Smith said he once paused for a moment on a street corner where the Salvation Army was holding an evening meeting. A lovely young woman stood in the circle singing a solo. Around her was the band—the drum, trombone, and cymbals. From the occasional notes he caught from the singer, he judged the girl had an exceptionally fine voice. He wanted to hear more of it, but the blare of the trumpet and the pounding of the drum smothered the solo and drowned out its beauty. So it is with the goodness of some people—they ruin the solo by the accompaniment. They do a good thing, and then spoil it by some ugly twist of the spirit. They faithfully perform some fine service in the church but grumble so much about it, seek their own interests in it, or want so much public recognition for it that you cannot hear the solo for what goes along with it, and you have the feeling they are not doing it for the sake of Christ but for their own.

It has been suggested that this respectable elder brother was the reason the prodigal left home, and the chief reason why he was so long coming back. It was easier for him to face his father than to face this fellow who stayed at home. Kipling put it in swashbuckling style; he makes the prodigal say:

> "I never was very refined, you see,
> (And it weighs on my brother's mind, you see,)
> But there's no reproach among swine, d'you see,
> For being a bit of a swine.
> So I'm off with wallet and staff to eat
> The bread that is three parts chaff to wheat,
> But glory be!—there's a laugh to it,
> Which isn't the case when we dine."
>
> *The Prodigal Son, from Kim,* by Rudyard Kipling. Copyright by Rudyard Kipling, reprinted by permission of Doubleday & Co., Inc., and Mrs. George Bambridge

Homes are often broken by that. "Incompatibility" is the lawyers' word for the offensive nagging of people who are smugly moral and piously unbending. God save us from a stuffed-shirt morality! It is not enough to be good; to be Christian we must be good in a nice way.

But now we must go deeper, for what we are talking about is no surface matter. It was Professor Drummond who first pointed out that these two sons are illustrations of two definite kinds of sin—the sins of passion in the younger and the sins of disposition in the elder. That goes to the heart of it. This boy who left home was simply giving in, as multitudes like him give in now, to the coarser sins of the flesh—to appetite, intemperance and the call of the world. "He wasted his substance in riotous living." The son who stayed at home betrayed those subtler sins of the spirit which are harder to get at and easier to hide and often more monstrous in consequence. His were the sins of envy, prejudice, bad temper, self-centeredness and social callousness. "He was angry and would not go in."

It is notorious how we see-saw between these two disfigurements and pit them against each other, excusing one or the other according to which happens to be our own particular weakness. It is popular in the movies, for example, to glorify the younger prodigal, glamorize his escapades and make his sins quite attractive and exciting. We have some writers who just love to poke fun at Puritan conventions; they make a point of picturing the broad-minded virtues of breezy Bohemians against the narrow meanness of stuffy churchmen and pious parsons; they leave the impression that the most charitable, likable people are the irreligious, who have thrown away the Book, and that, after all, the sins of the flesh are really quite harmless and of minor consequence. Drunkenness is such a peccadillo, gambling is not anything, and neither is profanity. As for sex expression, anything goes; marriage is a social convenience. Tolerance—*that's* the virtue! Just be good to your old grandmother and your kindheartedness will cover all your moral and minor irregularities.

The picture, of course, is utterly false and lopsided, a rationalization of prodigals in the far country who have canceled the father's right to rule. Anyone who can defend the moral corruption of our day in the name of tolerance or broadmindedness, who can look without concern on the misery that follows in the wake of lust and liquor and the disintegration of decency, is a lopsided person whose eyes are clouded and whose moral sensitiveness is all but dead. Never excuse the prodigal, in the Bible or in yourself.

On the other hand, we must deal with the elder brother too, and it should be frankly confessed that the emphasis of the Church has been lopsided in this direction. That is, the Church has attached more guilt to the sins of passion than to the subtler sins of disposition. We have been harder on profanity than on prejudice. If a man is habitually profane, we do not regard him as a Christian; but if all that is wrong with him is that he holds Negroes or people of other races and classes

168

in contempt, that is a minor deflection. Actually, this sin is more serious than the first. We have denounced drunkenness more than stinginess. We have regarded adultery as the major sin in immorality. When our forefathers spoke of a woman's virtue, they had reference almost exclusively to her chastity.

In a recent book there is the story of a young woman who lived in a small town. Her first baby was born too early, and the simple folk of the church would never forget it nor let her forget it, and while she had a lovely voice, she could not sing in the choir, though some who did sing in the choir were no match for her fine spirit. Thus they came to reverse the attitude of Jesus. One of the real weaknesses of Protestantism now in a world that demands large social vision is this lopsidedness—the notion that one is a Christian when he gets converted just far enough to be saved from his vices.

The Protestant movement came into being as a protest against corruption in the Medieval Church. Over against the moral laxity of the Roman Church, Protestantism exalted the personal virtues—purity, sobriety, honesty. With its emphasis on individual worth, it was an ideal faith for the common man, and it made a considerable contribution to the building of this nation. In his book, *The Rise of Capitalism,* Tawny traces the influence of the Reformation on the thinking of our Puritan forefathers. Protestantism, by stressing the virtues of thrift, hard work, temperance, and individual enterprise, produced an uncompromising conscience, developed exactly the kind of economic push our stern forefathers needed to grapple with the wilderness. They were a pretty good breed, even though they didn't laugh much—earnest men who kept the Commandments and saw that others kept them too.

The trouble was that the Reformation stopped too soon; it didn't follow through to develop the social conscience, and it made too little attempt to check the elder-brother kind of sinning. The result was that while the Church, by and large, sat in judgment on its members as to whether they smoked, gambled, drank, cursed, or kept the Sabbath (or, in some cases, wore buttons on their coats), it also permitted, at the same time, certain antisocial systems to take root in America. Slavery was one of them. It was unchristian to gamble, but not unchristian to own slaves. They also permitted the piling up of huge fortunes by robber barons who, as Dr. Sockman has said, kept the Sabbath and the Commandments and about everything else they could get their hands on. That is in our history and our heritage; we have a tendency to think of salvation solely in terms of personal virtue.

But, two wars in a generation have rudely awakened us to the realization that personal virtue is not enough, that this elder-brother kind of sinning—prejudice, social callousness—is what puts chaos into the world. And that it is quite possible to be sober and thrifty and decent, to stay at home and keep the rules, yet be utterly unchristian in social attitudes and in the fundamental outlook on the meaning of life.

Some years ago a well-known radio comedienne on the radio dramatized the Garden of Eden story. She made quite a burlesque of Eve and the apple. From all sections of the nation arose a profound moral protest to her sponsors, and the National Broadcasting Company banned her program from the air on the grounds that it was obscene and profane. Whereupon the buxom lady protested. "Profane!" she snorted. "There wasn't a word of profanity in it." And, of course, she was right. There were no cuss words. What she lacked was the moral insight to see that the whole thing was obscene and profane in its theme, its spirit, and its central purpose.

So it is with many who stay at home and keep the rules and sometimes get elected to church boards. They don't drink or curse or go to the dog races. But so far as their insight into the larger purposes for which Christ died is concerned, they seem almost blind, and indeed often repeat in their social attitude the same sins that conspired to put Him on a cross. So what we have in this parable is not one prodigal but two— one who sinned himself away from the father by the sins of passion, the other who sinned himself away from the father by the sins of disposition. Both of them stood in need of the forgiveness of God.

That brings us to the final word, and it is disturbing. Boil down the sins of this bad-tempered elder brother and you can label him with one word—"*lovelessness*." Respectable as he was, he had no love in him; he lacked the one thing without which, Paul said, all other virtues are worthless—"as sounding brass, or a tinkling cymbal"—the one thing that the New Testament keeps saying is the mark of a Christian and the test of sonship. "How can we love God whom we have not seen if we love not our brother whom we have seen?" The elder brother had no love in him. He could not use the word "brother." Had you noticed that? He said, "Thy son."

The home-coming that gladdened his father's heart stirred him to jealousy and anger. "He was angry and would not go in." He stood outside hearing the music, sulking about the fuss being made over a wastrel, deep in his callous heart resenting his father's happiness and his brother's return. And when his father remonstrated with him, he blew up. "I stay at home. I do the work. I obey you. I keep myself respectable. You make no fuss over me. But when this, thy son, is come . . ." Thy son! He could not say "brother." And it shut him out. The curtain closes on the story with the younger prodigal inside the father's house and the elder brother outside.

That is why, when we let our mind dwell on this story, we wonder about some people who stay at home and keep the rules and feel pretty satisfied with themselves. We wonder, too, about the soul of America today with this cry coming in from all the far countries of the earth—the cry for light, for bread, for God. We are decent people here, well fed, thrifty, industrious, respectable; yet we are somewhat calloused to catastrophe, not wanting to be disturbed much, not caring much about troubled people or whether or not they get home to God from the far country of their misery. "Don't bother us with it. Don't keep passing a collection box to us. Don't irritate us with their troubles."

Well, the elder brother was shut out with that. That is all that was wrong with him—social callousness. He could not say "brother" to his brother. Disclaiming kinship with his problem brother, he lost sonship with his father and by lovelessness he shut himself out of the father's house. That is where Jesus drew the line between those who were with Him and those who were against Him.

Isn't it odd that that is precisely where the lines are being drawn now, in this shrinking earth? We have to say "brother" now, have to say it to some very unlovable people, have to say it or perish, have to say it or be shut out not only from heaven but from peace and a decent future as well. That is what life is telling us. We have to say "brother." We can't be loveless any more, or callous. We can't be elder brothers any more and stay alive. Literally, it has come to pass that there is no salvation except we repent of the elder brother brand of sinning, join hands across all barriers with all men, and say, "Brother." And we must do it quickly or be shut out.

What we must have in the church is a bigger evangelism, an evangelism that not only calls the prodigal in from his wanderings but one that also redeems from unbrotherliness and un-Christ likeness the prodigals who stay decently at home.

One night, in an old-fashioned evangelistic meeting, the

172

minister had called for those who felt the need of prayer to linger after the service at the altar of the church. In the quiet, came a number, among them two men from opposite sides of the church. Without notice of each other, they knelt at the altar to pray. When, after a few moments, they arose, they looked at each other in startled recognition. When before they had faced each other one was a judge pronouncing sentence, the other a man who, in the frailties of his flesh, had run afoul of the law. Here, however, at the altar of the church, before the higher tribunal of Christ's spirit, they both stood in common need. And in the bountiful mercy of God they clasped hands in the common fraternity of the forgiven.

So we leave the great parable with the definite feeling that our Lord was talking about us. If He missed us in the first part He reached us in the second; and over it all is still the boundless love of the Father within whose house our restless souls find their true home.